JOHN CHRYSOSTOM

JOHN CHRYSOSTOM

An Introduction to His Life and Thought

SAMANTHA L. MILLER

 CASCADE *Books* • Eugene, Oregon

JOHN CHRYSOSTOM
An Introduction to His Life and Thought

Copyright © 2026 Samantha L. Miller. All rights reserved. Except for brief quotations in critical publications or reviews, no part of this book may be reproduced in any manner without prior written permission from the publisher. Write: Permissions, Wipf and Stock Publishers, 199 W. 8th Ave., Suite 3, Eugene, OR 97401.

Cascade Books
An Imprint of Wipf and Stock Publishers
199 W. 8th Ave., Suite 3
Eugene, OR 97401

www.wipfandstock.com

PAPERBACK ISBN: 978-1-6667-7033-9
HARDCOVER ISBN: 978-1-6667-7034-6
EBOOK ISBN: 978-1-6667-7035-3

Cataloguing-in-Publication data:

Names: Miller, Samantha L. [author].

Title: John Chrysostom : an introduction to his life and thought / by Samantha L. Miller.

Description: Eugene, OR: Cascade Books, 2026 | Series: Cascade Companions | Includes bibliographical references and index.

Identifiers: ISBN 978-1-6667-7033-9 (paperback) | ISBN 978-1-6667-7034-6 (hardcover) | ISBN 978-1-6667-7035-3 (ebook)

Subjects: LCSH: John Chrysostom, Saint, –407 | Christian saints—Byzantine Empire—Biography. | Theology—History—Early church, ca. 30–600.

Classification: BR65.C46 M555 2026 (paperback) | BR65.C46 (ebook)

01/28/26

For Rod, Tryg, Tara, Chuck, Mack, Jeremy, Kent, Mark, Don Deena, Scott, and Liv
—the best pastors I have known and the best preachers I have sat under, "Golden Mouths" every one of you

CONTENTS

List of Abbreviations | ix
Acknowledgments | xiii
Introduction: Why Should Anyone Care About John Chrysostom? | 1

PART 1: CHRYSOSTOM'S LIFE

1. Chrysostom's Biography | 9
2. Chrysostom's World | 25

PART 2: CHRYSOSTOM'S THOUGHT

3. Pastoral Theology | 43
4. Asceticism | 61
5. Virtue, or the Christian Life | 75
6. Almsgiving, Wealth, and Poverty | 90
7. Salvation | 107
8. Problems | 122

Conclusion | 141
Bibliography | 149
Index of Chrysostom's Works | 157

LIST OF ABBREVIATIONS

GENERAL

ANF	*Ante-Nicene Fathers* Series
Dial.	Palladius, *Dialogue on the Life of John Chrysostom*
GNO	Gregorii Nysseni Opera
NPNF[1]	*Nicene and Post-Nicene Fathers*, First Series
NPNF[2]	*Nicene and Post-Nicene Fathers*, Second Series
PG	Patrologia Graeca
PO	Patrologia Orientalis
SC	Sources chrétiennes

CHRYSOSTOM'S WORKS

Adv. Jud.	Adversus Judaeos	Discourses Against Judaizing Christians
Catech. illum.	Catecheses ad illuminandos	Homilies to Those About to Be Baptized
Comm. Job	Commentarius in Job	Commentary on Job

List of Abbreviations

Comp. reg. mon.	Comparatio regis et monachi	Comparison Between a King and a Monk
Diab.	De diabolo tentatore	On the Powers of the Devil
Eleem.	De eleemosyna	On Almsgiving
Ep. Olymp.	Epistulae ad Olympiadem	Letters to Olympias
Exp. Ps.	Expositiones in Psalmos	Expositions on the Psalms
Hom. 1 Cor.	Homiliae in epistulam i ad Corinthios	Homilies on 1 Corinthians
Hom. 2 Cor.	Homiliae in epistulam ii ad Corinthios	Homilies on 2 Corinthians
Hom. Col.	Homiliae in epistulam ad Colossenses	Homilies on Colossians
Hom. Eph.	Homiliae in epistulam ad Ephesios	Homilies on Ephesians
Hom. Gal.	Homiliae in epistulam ad Galatas commentaries	Commentary on Galatians
Hom. Gen.	Homiliae in Genesim	Homilies on Genesis
Hom. Heb.	Homiliae in epistulam ad Hebraeos	Homilies on Hebrews
Hom. Jo.	Homiliae in Joannem	Homilies on John
Hom. Matt.	Homiliae in Matthaeum	Homilies on Matthew
Hom. Phil.	Homiliae in epistulam ad Philippenses	Homilies on Philippians
Hom. Rom.	Homiliae in epistulam ad Romanos	Homilies on Romans
Hom. 1 Tim.	Homiliae in epistulam i ad Timotheum	Homilies on 1 Timothy
Laed.	Quod nemo laeditur nisi a se ipso	No One Can Harm the One Who Does Not Harm Himself

List of Abbreviations

Laz.	De Lazaro	On Lazarus and the Rich Man
Oppugn.	Adversus oppugnatores vitae monasticae	Against the Opponents of the Monastic Life
Paenit.	De paenitentia	On Penitence
Sac.	De sacerdotio	On the Priesthood
Scand.	Ad eos qui scandalizati sunt	On Providence
Stat.	Ad populum Antiochenum de statuis	On the Statues
Vid.	Ad viduam juniorem	Letter to a Young Widow

ACKNOWLEDGMENTS

THE IMPETUS OF THIS book was not Wipf and Stock's editor Dr. Robin Parry approaching me to write this volume of the Cascade Companion series, though I owe Robin much gratitude for seeking me out and persuading me to write this for them, as well as for his help in bringing the volume to print. No, this book would never have happened at all were it not for Rev. Dr. Trygve Johnson and Dr. Kristen Johnson hosting the Pre-Seminary Society in their living room when I was a student at Hope College twenty years ago. There they invited Dr. Jerry Sittser to speak with their nerdiest of students. Jerry mentioned John Chrysostom's *On the Priesthood*, and I found it in the library and read it the next day. That's how Chrysostom and I became friends, so Tryg, Kristen, and Jerry are the ones who get the biggest thanks for this work.

Much more recently, I am grateful to Whitworth University for their support of this project through summer research fellowships and a mini-sabbatical as well as to Provost John Pell for his annual writing retreat, which provided a week of early summer to spur me into writing alongside colleagues with meals and conversations. Additionally, I have John to thank for setting me straight about the curricula of ancient rhetorical schools.

Acknowledgments

A few dear friends undertook to read the manuscript and give me feedback: Paul Utterback, Jake Jacobs, Sarah Emerson, and Carolyn McCarthy. Their comments challenged me to make the book both richer and more accessible. Some of these friends were those I kept in mind as I wrote—this is for you and your curiosity about this weird guy I study and this weird work I do.

I have been fortunate to sit under so many preachers and pastors who are the vocational descendants of the master John Chrysostom, and I am grateful always for the care you have taken with your work, the care you have taken of and for me, and the care you have taken with words. Rod Kalajainen, Tryg Johnson, Tara Spuhler McCabe, Chuck Campbell, Mack Dennis, Jeremy Troxler, Kent Busman, Mark McDonough, Don Deena Johnson, Scott Kisker, and Liv Andrews: I have gotten to know Christ through you. Thank you.

To my parents and my brother, thank you for all the various kinds of support you have given me to make both my life and my career possible.

Finally, thank you to so many dear friends who are the joy of my life: Chris Jager; Erin Engstrom; Melissa Brandes; Sarah Kinglet; Josey and Connor Brady; Kent and Jill Busman; Liv, Casey, Arlo, and Robin Andrews; Jonathan and Stacey Moo; Jeff Meyers; Nathan and Lisa Lunsford; Kate and Ryan Hemmer; Anne Carpenter; Jakob Rinderknecht; Chuck Green; Mark and Maggie McDonough; Kristen and Trygve Johnson; Scott and Roberta Kisker; Stephen Waers; Nathan Willowby; Warren Smith; Olivia Cope; Mary Miller; Heather James; Amanda Clark; Elizabeth Abbey; and Nicole Sheets. For everything from encouragement while I cry about how hard being human is to meals at just the right time (or any time!) to bad puns to laughter that makes our faces hurt to early morning canoe paddles, you all have sustained me and made life very rich indeed. I look forward to an eternity of these things together.

INTRODUCTION

Why Should Anyone Care About John Chrysostom?

I BECAME FRIENDS WITH John Chrysostom as a sophomore in college.[1] I met him when a visiting professor told a group I belonged to that Chrysostom's *On the Priesthood* was one of the best books on pastoral theology and that it still read as though it were written yesterday, not sixteen hundred years ago. The next day I read the book in a sitting and discovered in John a kindred spirit, someone also more afraid of his call than awed by it. I decided then that we would be good friends.

I have come to know John well since then, and just as with all of my living friends, he has some traits and tendencies that I find more endearing than others, some ideas that are wise and enduring, from which I have learned and been edified, and other ideas that I forgive him for or which I

---

1. The fact that I did not think it strange to be making friends with a (long) dead man should probably have tipped me off to my vocation as a historical theologian.

ignore. Also as with my living friends, I think he is amazing and everyone should know him. I want all of my friends to be friends. So, in that sense, this is an introduction. Let me introduce you, dear reader, to my friend John Chrysostom.

My students tell me that just because I think someone is interesting or even fascinating does not, in fact, always make that person interesting, fascinating, relevant, or someone they think they should care about. They do not usually say this in so many words. Usually they just give me a look. But I am now practiced at making a case for their knowing whichever dead friend I am about to introduce them to. Why should anyone care about John Chrysostom? Let me count the ways.

First, John Chrysostom was a preacher. A very good one. Most of the writings we have from him are sermons, so he is expounding Scripture and practically addressing how to live a Christian life. Moreover, as we will see, he is concerned with many of the same things that most Christians are still concerned with: how to think about and use money, how to deal with suffering, how to raise children well, what it means to live like Christ, that Christ is redeeming the world and us, even how to think about and use emotion well. Though we are chronologically and culturally distant from Chrysostom, theologically we are near. We believe in the same God. We are reading the same Scripture. The same Holy Spirit is living and working within each of us. The things Chrysostom preaches about are the things we care about as we attempt to live Christian lives. Chrysostom, though, was identified as someone whose understanding of Scripture and the Christian life was especially astute, perhaps even guided by the Spirit for more people than just those of his own time, and for the last sixteen hundred years, people have continued to agree that Chrysostom's words were worth keeping around. We look to him as an older, wiser brother in faith just as we look to our own living mentors.

Because he was a preacher, concerned with guiding laypeople more than writing doctrinal treatises and sorting out the details of Christian belief, he is speaking to *us*. He is concerned most with daily Christian living, just as we are. We are the very people he has in mind, and the Holy Spirit can still speak to us through his words just as much as the Spirit spoke to those who heard the words in his original congregation. If we believe in the communion of saints, the cloud of witnesses, then Chrysostom is one of the many we need to listen to.

Additionally, because he was a preacher and was preaching to laity rather than professional theologians, his writing, his thoughts, are accessible. Reading John Chrysostom does not require years of study in theology or acquaintance with esoteric ideas or even, for the most part, knowledge of another language (a lot of Chrysostom's material has been translated into English, French, and German). Anyone who is interested in what it means to follow God in this world can pick up Chrysostom's sermons and read them, understand them, perhaps even integrate them into their own lives. Chrysostom's, "Pay attention to prayer!" and "Pay attention not only to the words [of the sermon] but also when at home in your house constantly read the Scriptures" are for us too.[2]

Finally, Chrysostom gives us a window into fourth-century Christianity. The church has looked different in different times and places, and we only see a whole picture of the church when we see all the different ways it has been. There are things we can leave in the past as part of a cultural moment or historical trend, but there are also real truths about Christ mediated by every instantiation of his body.

2. *Hom. Heb.* 27.5 (PG 63:189); *Laz.* 3.1 (PG 48:991–2).

Chrysostom as preacher in Antioch, Syria (modern-day Antakya in southern Turkey; the ancient region of Syria includes areas that are now in Turkey) and then bishop in Constantinople (modern-day Istanbul, Turkey), in the late fourth century, gives us a glimpse of the church in that time and those places.

Through his sermons and some treatises, we see what worship was like; we see what concerned "average" Christians, or at least what clergy were concerned for among average Christians; through Chrysostom's complaints and urgings we see what did *not* concern average Christians. For example, Chrysostom often yelled at his congregants for going to theaters and horse races instead of worship ("The day before yesterday [when we were talking about Scripture], others took places in theaters, watching the devil's show!"), suggesting that many average Christians were concerned more with entertainment than worship.[3] But since we do not have writings from these average Christians, we do not know whether they would agree with their preacher's assessment of their concerns. Because Chrysostom was a theologian in his own right we see what issues concerned the church after the Councils of Nicaea and Constantinople defined the nature of the Trinity. After heavy debate, what mattered to people? Because Chrysostom was concerned about virtue and the ascetic life, we glimpse the ancient Syrian Christians living in caves and what they can teach Christians in the cities.

So why should anyone care about John Chrysostom? Because he is someone God used to offer some wisdom to those of us in the pews every Sunday. I, at least, know I still need a lot of wisdom.

The way I will introduce Chrysostom is in two chapters about his life and then six chapters exploring significant

---

3. *Diab.* 2.1 (SC 560:154–56).

Introduction

themes in his thought. Chapter 1 is a basic biography. What did Chrysostom do in his life and in what order? What events shaped him? Who were his friends and enemies? This chapter provides an overview of Chrysostom's life so we start with an understanding of who the man was. Chapter 2 offers a description of the world Chrysostom lived and preached in. Fourth-century Antioch and Constantinople were places of culture and extremes in wealth and poverty, Constantinople was the place of imperial power, and Chrysostom's congregation would have been mixed in terms of gender, socioeconomic class, and ethnicity. Knowing both Chrysostom's life and world help us understand his preaching and thought better.

Chapter 3 is about Chrysostom's pastoral theology, what he thinks being a pastor (in his language, a priest) is all about. In short, being a priest is about being a physician of souls. He preaches the healing words of Scripture like medicine for the sin-sick soul. Chapter 4 explores Chrysostom's emphasis on asceticism—a life of self-restraint for the purpose of greater attachment to God—throughout his life. Chrysostom holds up monks as exemplars of Christian living that he wants everyone to follow even when they live in the cities. The ability to hold things of this world loosely is the aim of asceticism, and Chrysostom says that this way of detachment allows a person to live in relationship with God in the way humans were intended to in the garden in the beginning.

Chapter 5 looks at Chrysostom's near-constant exhortations to virtue, or right living. Chrysostom believed that virtue is each person's particular responsibility because each person has been created with a faculty of choice that is free and self-determining. As long as no one else can force a person to do anything, both her virtue and her vice are her responsibility alone, and therefore, a person is supposed to

Introduction

be virtuous. Virtue is what a Christian contributes to her salvation. Chapter 6 discusses Chrysostom's heavy insistence on almsgiving. He so strongly tells his congregants to give away their money that he sometimes sounds like almsgiving is a means of salvation. The important pieces here for him are that Christians ought to meet the needs of those around them, that wealth is an external circumstance that does not indicate either the virtue or the sin of the person, and that a Christian needs to hold money loosely in order to be better focused on God.

Chapter 7 ties many of these themes together in a discussion of Chrysostom's understanding of salvation. Chrysostom has a cooperative vision of salvation. For him, God does all the primary work and heavy lifting of salvation in Christ's incarnation, death, and resurrection, but Christians need to contribute their faith and their virtue. Finally, chapter 8 explores two major problematic themes in Chrysostom's thought: his views on women and his anti-Semitism. These are aspects of Chrysostom's thought that I do not think we should emulate, but they exist and I need to acknowledge them, if only as a way, as a Christian, to take responsibility for them and help the church grow in more holiness. This will also lead us into a discussion about how to read ancient sources or anyone we disagree with and how we discern truth in these conversations.

Along the way I include discussion questions at the end of each chapter that I hope will provoke more conversation. The goal of this book is to provide a mere *introduction* to John Chrysostom and his thought, to whet the appetite for more investigation, reading, and conversation about what he might have to offer Christians today. So without further ado, let me tell you about my friend, John.

PART 1
CHRYSOSTOM'S LIFE

1

CHRYSOSTOM'S BIOGRAPHY

EARLY LIFE

CHRYSOSTOM IS NOT HIS last name. It is his nickname, meaning "the golden mouth," or "the golden tongue," and people called him that because of his extraordinary skill in preaching. But when he was born in Antioch in 347 CE, he was born John. In his time and place, people did not have or use surnames. He would have been known in his community as John the son of Secundus and Anthusa, the younger brother of a sister whose name we do not remember. His father seems to have been a civil servant high up in the government, which means he was probably wealthy, and he was probably a Roman citizen, and we know that at least his mother was a Christian. His father died shortly after Chrysostom's birth, and his mother, who did not remarry, raised the boy as a Christian.[1]

---

1. What we know of Chrysostom's biography comes primarily

PART 1: CHRYSOSTOM'S LIFE

Because his parents had high social standing, Chrysostom enjoyed the standard education for noble boys of his time: what we would consider elementary school, then grammar school, where he learned Greek classic literature, and then from about fourteen on he entered a school of rhetoric under Libanius, a famous pagan orator. Rhetoric was reserved for children of nobles, since they were not required to earn money to help sustain the family. Under Libanius, Chrysostom learned the arts of writing and public speaking. He would have trained by memorizing and reciting classical Greek texts; writing debates and other exercises of his own for correction, often writing to imitate Libanius's own works, since imitation was understood to be the primary method of learning; and analysis of classical Greek texts for how the rhetoric functioned.[2] Libanius seems to have especially focused on training students to use praise and invective in their orations. In short, Chrysostom was learning to argue and persuade, skills that because of his facility with them would lead to his designation as the Golden Mouth.[3] According to Chrysostom's biographer So-

---

from three ancient biographies: Sozomen of Gaza's *Ecclesiastical History*, Socrates of Constantinople's *Ecclesiastical History*, and Palladius's *Dialogue on the Life of John Chrysostom*. Critical editions: Sozomen, *Histoire ecclésiastique: Livres VII–IX*, vol. 4; Socrates of Constantinople, *Histoire ecclésiastique: IV–VI*, vol. 3; Palladius, *Dialogue sur la vie de Jean Chrysostome*, vol. 1. English translations: Sozomen and Socrates both: Schaff et al., *NPNF*[2] 2:137–52 (Sozomen); 2:398–418 (Socrates); Palladius, *Dialogue* (trans. Meyer). For a modern biography, the standard work is Kelly, *Golden Mouth*. In addition, we have an anonymous funerary speech for John Chrysostom, which is apologetic and laudatory in nature: Wallraff, *Ps.-Martyrius: Oratio funebris in laudem sancti Iohannis Chrysostomi*. English: Barnes and Bevans, *Funerary Speech for John Chrysostom*.

2. Two good introductions to rhetorical schools of the ancient world are Bizzell and Herzberg, *Rhetorical Tradition*; and Kennedy, *Progymnasmata*.

3. For more on the rhetorical training Chrysostom received

zomen, Libanius said that Chrysostom was greater than all of the other orators of his time.[4]

While in Libanius's school, Chrysostom was not yet baptized but would have been attending church regularly. The practice of baptism was a serious thing at that time, requiring a three-year period of learning Christian doctrine and being mentored by a more mature Christian into the church's ways of life. To choose baptism was to choose this particular way of life. One was then allowed to participate in the Eucharist at worship but was required to give up anything considered to be sinful. Studying among pagans, and like the other young men of his time (and ours), Chrysostom loved the entertainments available to him: theater and chariot races and other sundry pursuits discouraged by preachers of the day. He was not ready for baptism yet; he enjoyed these pursuits too much.

Chrysostom intended to become a civil servant like his father had been, which was the course his training was preparing him for, but when his friend Basil and his close association with Bishop Meletios persuaded him to become serious about his religion, there was no looking back. At about twenty he was baptized, left the path set out by Libanius (Libanius wrote of his disappointment. When asked who should succeed him, he wrote: "John, if the Christians had not plundered him from us"),[5] and devoted himself with all intensity to his faith.

---

under Libanius, see Cribiore, *School of Libanius*. Many of our famous Christian writers and theologians of the time also trained at rhetorical schools, some also under Libanius. Basil of Caesarea famously wrote an argument for why Christian young men should bother learning rhetoric, even though it was pagan. See Basil the Great, *Address to Young Men on Greek Literature*.

4. Sozomen, *Ecclesiastical History* 8.2 (SC 516:235; *NPNF*[2] 2:399–400).

5. Sozomen, *Ecclesiastical History* 8.2 (SC 516:235).

ASCETIC ENDEAVORS

Once Chrysostom made the decision to be baptized, he applied himself vigorously to the practice of his faith. Chrysostom seems to have been an intense personality: driven, zealous, perhaps even rigid. His sermons often suggest that being a Christian is an all-or-nothing endeavor. If one is not doing things that follow Christ, then one is following the devil. For example, he preaches, "Do you see the unquenchable fire prepared for [the devil], and for us, unless we are lazy, the kingdom? Then let us consider these things and take charge of our lives. Let us flee evil and never be victim to the devil's machinations."[6] Some of this can be attributed to the sermonic form—he is trying to persuade his congregation to live in a particular way, and the art of persuasion can intensify any given statement. However, other rhetoricians of a similar time, such as Gregory of Nyssa and Augustine, come across less rigid, so some of Chrysostom's intensity seems to be temperament. It was not enough for him, once baptized, to attend church on Sunday mornings and pray regularly. Chrysostom wanted to be an ascetic, another word for a monk. The height of Christian practice at the time, those considered to be the true athletes of God, were the ascetics, especially those living in the mountains outside the city. I'll discuss this in more depth in chapter 4, but for now it is enough to note that this was Chrysostom's desire: to give himself fully to God in this extreme living. His mother, however, desired that he stay home and continue to live with her.

Chrysostom stayed with his mother until her death but managed to live a form of ascetic life with some other young men, including his friend Basil, nearby while at home. Together they apprenticed themselves to Diodore,

---

6. *Hom. Gen.* 17.6 (PG 53:141).

one of the primary teachers in the theological school of Antioch and in how to read Scripture. There he learned both the ascetic way of life and how to interpret Scripture, since his training had all been focused on classical Greek texts to this point. Chrysostom and these young men lived in their separate homes but met together for prayer and Bible study. They committed to celibacy and fasting from meat and wine and wore clothes that marked them apart as practicing ascetics. They also assisted the local clergy in worship and with other pastoral and administrative duties.[7]

During this time Chrysostom wrote two pieces that are among his earliest works: *Comparison Between a King and a Monk* and *Letter to Theodore*.[8] These in particular show Chrysostom's zeal for the ascetic life and give us a glimpse of both his early rhetoric and his temperament. *Comparison* extols the ways a monk is living a more desirable life than a king, and *To Theodore* charges Chrysostom's friend Theodore to return to the ascetic life he left. Theodore, later to become the bishop of Mopsuestia, was one of the friends in their small ascetic community who had decided to leave in order to marry, and he was struggling with despair. Chrysostom tells his friend that the devil is distracting him, tempting him away from the life to which he had committed himself and rooting the despair in him. But, says Chrysostom, Theodore can return to God. Return to the ascetic life, which is the way of committed Christians, and God and Theodore's brothers in the community will welcome him back.[9] The over-the-top language

---

7. Kelly, *Golden Mouth*, 20.

8. John Chrysostom, *Comparison and Against the Opponents*; John Chrysostom, *A Theodore* (ed. Dumortier). English translation of the letter: Habib, *On Repentance and Defeating Despair*.

9. Blake Leyerle has an interesting analysis of Chrysostom's rhetorical technique in this letter as stirring up emotions of fear in

Chrysostom uses to describe the benefits and goods of the ascetic life as well as its superiority to all worldly forms of life (marriage, civil office, and so on) show us his youthful zeal for and commitment to the most rigorous way of life he can imagine to be a Christian.

Around 370, after three years as Bishop Meletios's personal aide, Chrysostom was made an official reader in the church. Shortly after this, in 372, which was some time after Chrysostom's mother passed, Chrysostom retreated into a semi-communal monasticism with the monks on Mt. Silpios outside the city. In fact, shortly after his reception as an official reader, leaders of the church decided to ordain him and his friend Basil to the priesthood. At the time it was not unusual for church leadership to kidnap those they thought best suited to be priests and ordain them by force. Chrysostom got wind of the plan and hid, running away to the monks, which is what he had always wanted to do.[10] He lived there in apprenticeship to an elderly Syrian expert in the ascetic life. They worshiped, fasted, prayed, studied Scriptures, held silence, and engaged in some physical labor—weaving cloth or baskets or farming, the profits of which were given to the poor—all in an attempt to reach an uninterrupted communion with God.[11]

After four years, this semi-communal monasticism was no longer enough for Chrysostom, and he withdrew further into the mountain to become a hermit and live in rigorous solitude. For a little over two years, Palladius tells

---

Theodore to rouse him out of his *hrathymia* (ῥαθυμία), the primal sin and the sin that asceticism primarily combats. See Leyerle, *Narrative Shape of Emotion*, 135, 165.

10. Chrysostom's *On the Priesthood* is his defense of his actions at this time. Apparently Basil was livid with him for leaving him to be ordained alone.

11. For a full description of what this life would have entailed, see Kelly, *Golden Mouth*, 30–32.

us, Chrysostom rarely slept, never laid down, memorized both the Old and New Testaments, and fasted to an extreme. Indeed, it is this rigor of fasting, vigils, and the extreme cold he endured that ruined his bodily health.[12] It was so bad, in fact, that Chrysostom had to return to the city. To continue his asceticism would have killed him.

ORDINATION AND PRIESTLY ROLE IN ANTIOCH

When Chrysostom returned to the city, he received the ordination that church leadership still wanted to give him. It was a process. He spent two more years as a reader under Bishop Meletios, was ordained a deacon about 381, and then ordained a priest under Bishop Flavian in 386. He served twelve years at the church in Antioch, where his primary responsibility was preaching, followed by responsibilities for instructing the catechumens (those in the three-year process for baptism) before their baptisms at Easter each year as well as the various tasks related to administrating the church's property—tasks that Chrysostom complained about as taking him away from his pastoral care work. In addition, Bishop Flavian chose Chrysostom to be his personal aide, and so Chrysostom went with Flavian everywhere. Flavian was setting Chrysostom up to be his successor.

The sermons Chrysostom was famous for would have been preached after the Gospel reading, before the non-baptized audience members were dismissed and the baptized participated in Eucharist together. A stenographer took down the sermon in shorthand while Chrysostom

12. Palladius, *Dial.* 5 (SC 341:108–10; Meyer, 35). See also the account by ps-Martyrios in his funerary speech for John Chrysostom, where he does not mention any ill health but only says that God would not allow his chosen instrument to hide in the desert: Barnes and Bevans, *Funerary Speech for John Chrysostom*, 42.

preached, and then he revised them himself for publication afterward. To the best of our knowledge, Chrysostom was an extemporaneous preacher: he did not write out full sermons ahead of time but preached in the moment. With his mastery of Scripture—having memorized most of it while living as a monk in the mountains—he was able to draw together themes, passages, and ideas on the spot to illuminate or explore a passage. We see his improvisation especially in comments he makes about noticing absences, which he assumes are people frequenting the horse races rather than worship, or telling people to stop applauding, or warning against pickpockets he sees. Chrysostom would pick up some question or problem in the text just read, or some theme or controversy introduced by the text, and expound upon it with all the force of his rhetorical skill, often ending with a call to live some particular way in response. Very often those ending sections began, "Therefore let us not think too little of our salvation!"[13] Moreover, because the texts read in worship would be continuous week to week, for the most part Chrysostom would preach through a whole book of Scripture. One of the first sets of homilies he preached was on the book of Genesis (sixty-seven homilies).

All we have from this period are Chrysostom's writings, and his biographers do not comment further, so we have no clues about Chrysostom's personal life during this time or even any major events that he is involved in, with one exception. In the winter of 387, just before Lent, Antioch saw violent riots. The emperor had announced a heavy new tax that would affect all citizens, and riots broke out in protest. Among other vandalism, mobs attacked portraits and statues of the emperor, in many cases pulling them down and destroying them in the streets.[14] Various

13. *Hom. Gen.* 8.6 (PG 53:75–76).

14. Our two primary accounts of the riots are Chrysostom's

authorities put the riots down quickly, but as soon as people realized what they had done—defacing the emperor's image was equivalent to treason—they began to fear the emperor's retribution. Monks came down from the mountains into the cities to plead with the authorities on behalf of the accused citizens, and Chrysostom preached his *Homilies on the Statues* during Lent to try to calm the situation, sometimes extolling the emperor as a model Christian ruler, especially in his gracious and forgiving response to the people of Antioch.[15]

From this we see the public role Chrysostom had as priest in the city. Preaching was his main duty, and preaching was also a public event that could have an affect on the city or even imperial politics. We also see in this event that Chrysostom could be savvy about his position and his preaching in order to sway the emperor to leniency for the people. We know Chrysostom for his intensity and unyieldingness, his willingness to stand against the authorities when he understood it to be the right thing to do, and in general the narrative has been that Chrysostom was not especially politically savvy, or at least was unwilling to be. Yet in his emperor-flattering rhetoric in these homilies, it seems that Chrysostom was more canny than the story goes.[16]

---

twenty-one *Homilies on the Statues* and five of Libanius's *Orations* (19–23). See Chrysostom, *Stat.*, PG 49:15–223. English translation Schaff et al., NPNF[1] 9:317–489. Libanius, *Selected Orations, Volume II* (trans. Norman), 19–23, 30, 33, 45, 47–50, pp. 246–419.

15. *Stat.* 21.4 (PG 49:219–20).

16. Or perhaps he was simply less practiced. Kelly suggests that John grew in his confidence, in self-assertiveness, and in claims of authority for the role of priest during his years at Antioch. His early sermons have self-effacing rhetoric, but by 390 he is ordering deacons to expel unworthy communicants from the church. See Kelly, *Golden Mouth*, 100–101.

PART 1: CHRYSOSTOM'S LIFE

BISHOP OF CONSTANTINOPLE

Ecclesiastical authorities recognized Chrysostom's immense talents and his grooming from Flavian, and in early 398 ordained him bishop of Constantinople, the capital city of the Eastern Roman Empire.[17] He was preaching to the rich and powerful, including Emperor Arcadius and Empress Eudoxia, at Hagia Sophia, the Great Church. Also at this church Chrysostom met Olympias, the head of the convent attached to the Great Church, who would become his dear and spiritual friend. At this time Chrysostom was the only bishop in Constantinople, and there was no role of archbishop or patriarch until the Council of Chalcedon in 451. Although the bishop of Constantinople was not in any official capacity head of the Eastern church—he was meant to be simply one among all the bishops—because Constantinople was the capitol and the emperor was part of the congregation, the bishop of Constantinople was unofficially the head and functioned as the preeminent bishop. Chrysostom was thus the most powerful ecclesiastical authority in the East.

Though preaching and instruction remained his primary—and most public—duties as bishop, Chrysostom had additional administrative responsibilities, such as overseeing the churches and clergy in his area, overseeing the church's property, and advising the emperor. It seems that though people loved his preaching, he became unpopular and even hated by some because of the standards to which he held people. It was not uncommon for him to preach, "Let us . . . not neglect our own salvation, and let us give all

---

17. The Calendar of Constantinople gives Chrysostom's ordination date as December 15, 397, but Socrates records it as February 26, 398. Most scholars follow Socrates because he was always very precise. See Kelly, *Golden Mouth*, 106; and Socrates, *Ecclesiastical History* 6.2 (SC 505:260–64; *NPNF*² 2:138), for a full discussion.

attention to a godly way of life, knowing that on this most of all we will either be condemned or be deemed worthy of loving kindness from him."[18] Chrysostom was especially outspoken about the dangers of wealth: "Now, while we are being led on the road to hell, it is possible to be set free by giving away half of our possessions, we choose both punishment and to rashly hold fast to the possessions that are not ours."[19] Most people, especially his wealthy parishioners, did not want to get rid of half of their possessions, let alone hear that their refusal to give up so much would lead to hell.

It was not just his preaching that called up high moral standards, either. He made attempts to reform the clergy in his jurisdiction and even fired several who were not the quality he insisted on for such an important office. Other aspects of his reform included cutting excesses in the budget, which manifested as never hosting meals and often declining invitations to meals, something expected of the person in his position for the purposes of church and state relations. Ever the ascetic, however, Chrysostom insisted on restriction in both wealth and diet. Socrates of Constantinople reports that this was a special sore spot for dignitaries and goes so far as to question whether this was really a show of Chrysostom's asceticism or whether it was a power play.[20] Finally, though he did not make explicit criticism of the emperor in his sermons, he did sometimes come close and definitely made his position clear—that he as bishop had a final authority over the emperor, who was merely a

18. *In Hom. Gen.* 7.7 (PG 53:69).

19 *Hom. Jo.* 39.4 (PG 59:228).

20. Socrates, *Ecclesiastical History* 6.4. Sozomen also remarks on this issue, in *Ecclesiastical History* 8.9, and Palladius spends considerable time defending Chrysostom's lifestyle and reforms. Though Palladius is unapologetically on Chrysostom's side, the account does provide a list of complaints people had with Chrysostom. See Palladius, *Dial.* 6, 12–20 (SC 341:127–29, 231–451; Meyer, 40–41, 74–151).

temporal authority. Chrysostom said that he would excommunicate the emperor if that became necessary.

On the whole, Chrysostom stayed out of the political crises and issues of his day, something the empress did not appreciate. In the empress's view, the bishop role was to help and support rulers in their work of running a Christian empire. Chrysostom, in contrast, understood his primary duties to be pastoral. That said, he was often enough involved in the ecclesiastical struggles of his time, including a long trip to Asia to sort out a significant mess of clergy not doing their jobs.[21] Through this we glimpse Chrysostom's understanding of the role of bishop: overseer. His job was to shepherd the Christians of his city, and that sometimes included protecting them from false or dangerous shepherds. He preached and lived—as much as possible—the harshest sort of asceticism and virtue so as to encourage the transformation of the city into a truly Christian city.[22] In short, Chrysostom aimed to persuade all of his congregants to live virtuously, even to live angelic lives, so that the city would be a heavenly city.

TRIAL, EXILE, AND DEATH

The legend of Chrysostom's exile is that he offended and embarrassed Empress Eudoxia by pointing out her sin of luxury during a public sermon. The empress could not let

---

21. For a full account of the events, see Palladius, *Dial.* 13–16 (SC 341:273–303; Meyer, 88–98). Palladius gives the most thorough account, as he was present at key moments in the events. The other biographers give brief mention: Socrates, *Ecclesiastical History* 6.15 (SC 505:324–28; *NPNF*[2] 2:148–49); and Sozomen, *Ecclesiastical History* 8.6 (SC 516:263–67; *NPNF*[2] 2:403). See also Kelly, *Golden Mouth*, 163–80.

22. For a thorough treatment of Chrysostom's program for transformation, see Hartney, *John Chrysostom and the Transformation of the City*. For a shorter treatment, see Mitchell, "John Chrysostom."

that stand, so she had Chrysostom exiled. Very shortly after this decree, the empress suffered a miscarriage or some other misfortune, and Eudoxia interpreted this misfortune as punishment from God for exiling her bishop. Eudoxia called Chrysostom back to his pulpit, and soon enough Chrysostom called out the empress's sin again in a sermon. Eudoxia then had Chrysostom sent into exile a second time, and he died on one of the long marches, his body, already weakened from his extreme asceticism, unable to endure the harsh winter and the strenuous conditions of the march.

It is true that we have records of various conflicts between Eudoxia and Chrysostom, such as the time she stole a piece of land and Chrysostom referred to her as Jezebel stealing Naboth's vineyard.[23] However, that legend paints too simplistic—and unfair—a picture of Eudoxia and completely ignores the role of Theophilus, bishop of Alexandria, in the deposition and sentencing as well as the complex issues at play. Indeed, more recent scholarship has argued that Eudoxia, far from being a major player in Chrysostom's trial, was probably a moderating influence on Chrysostom's opponents.[24] It was Theophilus who remained the primary instigator.

In early 401, a group of refugee monks came to Constantinople seeking protection from Chrysostom. Referred to as the Long Brothers (or Tall Brothers) because of the notable height of their four leaders, they had been part of a community in Egypt founded by Evagrius. For a number of reasons involving political and ecclesiastical intrigue, as well as the accusation that they were followers of Origen's

23. Kelly discusses the legendary nature of this accusation and its probability as fact: Kelly, *Golden Mouth*, 170–71.

24. See Mayer, "Doing Violence to the Image of an Empress"; Liebeschuetz, *Barbarians and Bishops*.

theology,[25] the brothers were run out of one area after another by bishops, notably by Bishop Theophilus of Alexandria. Because of Theophilus's issues with Chrysostom—Chrysostom was chosen over Theophilus for the bishop's seat in Constantinople—Chrysostom was kind to the Long Brothers, but did not admit them to communion so as not to further provoke Theophilus. When the brothers complained directly to the emperor, the empress was sympathetic, got involved, and demanded that Theophilus come to court at Constantinople. This further fueled Theophilus's grievances with Chrysostom because he believed this meant that Chrysostom had more political favor than he did.

Ultimately Theophilus held the Synod of the Oak (403 CE), a trial of Chrysostom to depose him. The majority of the bishops present were from Egypt—and so sided with Theophilus rather than Chrysostom—and the remaining bishops present were chosen specifically because they were among Chrysostom's enemies. Among the twenty-nine charges were acts of violence, ill-treating clergy, wrongly deposing bishops, poor financial administration, and aspects of his personal life.[26] Most of the charges were patently false and many were petty, though given Chrysostom's severe way of ruling, there is probably some truth to some of them.

---

25. Origen was a third-century Christian thinker and writer especially well known for his allegorical ways of interpreting Scripture. In Chrysostom's time, various church authorities were concerned about parts of Origen's theology that seemed to say that all could be saved, including the devil, and that souls pre-existed before God created bodies to put them in.

26. For the full list, see Kelly, *Golden Mouth*, 221–22. The only record we have of the list is from Photios and Isaac the Monk, an appendix to Palladius's account: Palladius, *Dialogue sur la vie de Jean Chrysostome*, 2:100. No English available.

Chrysostom was found guilty and sentenced to exile. People protested, and Chrysostom was held outside the city. Pretty quickly the imperial court reversed its decision and brought Chrysostom back—it is unclear whether it was because there was an earthquake or a miscarriage or something else, but it seems the emperor and empress thought there was some divine retribution for Chrysostom's exile. More political intrigue followed for about a year, and then Chrysostom was again arrested shortly after Easter 404 and exiled for good.

During Chrysostom's exile, he wrote some 240 letters, including seventeen letters to Olympias, a wealthy widow who was one of his benefactors and his spiritual friend. In these letters we see both an example of his friendship and his gentler (for him) writing, his human side, as well as a sense of his own suffering. In one letter to Olympias, he writes of his suffering, "I finished these past two months no better than dead—and even worse. For I was living just enough to perceive the terrible things circling me everywhere. Everything was night to me—the day and the dawn and the middle of midday—and I spent every day nailed to my bed."[27] In another he encourages her: "Do not give yourself to the tyranny of despair, but prevail over the storm with reason. For you are able, and the wave is not greater than your skill."[28] These letters give some context to his own writing on suffering, especially in his *On Providence*, which he also writes during this time.

Chrysostom's already weakened health became worse over three winters, and the guards were instructed to move him to increasingly harsh places. He died on his forced march to Comana Pontica in 407. The guards buried him in the shrine of the martyr Basiliscus, where he had been staying.

27. *Ep. Olymp.* 12.1 (SC 13:316).
28. *Ep. Olymp.* 3b (SC 13:114).

PART 1: CHRYSOSTOM'S LIFE

DISCUSSION QUESTIONS

1. Though he lived sixteen hundred years ago, Chrysostom's story of trying to navigate the church and imperial politics feels very contemporary. What challenges do you see for Christians and church leaders trying to be faithful in your own political landscape? What can Chrysostom's example teach us?

2. Which part of Chrysostom's life did you most relate to? Why?

3. Chrysostom was not afraid to speak truth to power, and it eventually got him killed. How does this affect your own understanding of what it might mean to speak truth to power?

2

CHRYSOSTOM'S WORLD

For all that John Chrysostom is theologically near to us, he is chronologically distant. That distance is significant for having a better understanding of his writing and thought. People in history are not simply just like us but wearing funny clothes. Their mindsets are different; the foundational things they assume to be true about the world are often different. Those differences matter if we are to make sense of the things they speak and write. And so, this chapter provides a glimpse of the world in which Chrysostom lived, worked, preached, and ministered, as well as some context about the kinds of texts we still have from him. This background is important for understanding what Chrysostom thought and how we can use that thought today in edifying ways.

ANTIOCH

As I noted in the previous chapter, Chrysostom grew up in Antioch, lived as monk in the mountains just beyond the city walls, and received his ordination there. What was the city like? What culture formed him?

Antioch was the capital of the province of Syria in the Roman Empire (now south Turkey), a large city—somewhere between 150,000 and 300,000 people—smaller than Rome, but similar in size to Constantinople, though Constantinople grew much faster and overtook Antioch in prestige and significance by the end of the fourth century.[1] Antioch was a vibrant city, Greek in culture and language, though Syriac was the language of the peasants who farmed the land just beyond the city center. It was a place where 10 percent of people were considered the destitute poor, who lived in the open and relied on alms to survive; 80 percent of people were primarily artisans or small shopkeepers, who lived day to day rather than having property or savings and were always one step away from becoming the destitute poor; and 10 percent of people were wealthy landowners, who were insulated from issues of hunger, disease, and the more extreme forms of precarity.[2] Moreover, the destitute poor were on display everywhere and dependent on alms for necessities. Chrysostom's compassion for the poor was a major theme: "It is not the same to run past a beggar when you have seen him once or twice as it is to see him every day and not be moved by the continual sight to compassion and benevolence."[3]

Antioch was the "cultural capital of Asia Minor."[4] It was a prosperous city full of huge and ornate buildings, theaters, and an arena for horse races. Roman engineering and

---

1. The figures are from Liebeschuetz, *Antioch*, 92–96.

2. Berardino et al., *Encyclopedia of Ancient Christianity*, "Antioch of Syria, History."

3. *Laz.* 1.7 (PG 48:971).

4. Berardino et al., *Encyclopedia of Ancient Christianity*, "Antioch of Syria, Archaeology, Artistic Monuments."

the placement of the city on the bank of the Orontes River meant they had no shortage of water and boasted eighteen public baths. Just eight kilometers down the main road was Daphne, where its oracle and the famous temple of Apollo were, as well as the regular location of the Olympic games.[5]

Antioch's wealth came from a combination of being located on the region's commercial highway (between Asia and the Mediterranean), being connected to the nearby port, and the intense farming of the land surrounding the city. Antioch also had a mint and an arms factory, and between all of these things, the city had both wealth and goods. Intellectually, Antioch had a rich network of schools and teachers, like Libanius, as well as schools of Christian thought led by Diodore, Chrysostom, Theodore, and Theodoret. By Chrysostom's time it was considered a Christian city, though there were notable pagan and Jewish communities as well. It was also where the governor of Syria had his residence and was a military hub for the eastern part of the Roman Empire.

All of this luxury and the presence of the theaters, horse races, and Olympic games gave rise to Chrysostom's frequent admonitions against the common entertainments and to his frequent use of athletic contest imagery in homilies. The common entertainments were too accessible in his city and leading people astray—the Antiochenes generally had a reputation for being worldly and pleasure-seeking—and the games were accessible and therefore useful for metaphors and getting people to understand his point. Also forming Chrysostom's rhetorical context were the monks who lived in the mountains just outside the city, whom Chrysostom often held up as examples for his congregants to emulate.

---

5. Kelly, *Golden Mouth*, 1.

In Chrysostom's time there were three churches: the Old Church, the Great or Golden Church, and the Church of St. Babylas.[6] The first two were in the city and used for regular worship; the last was further out and mainly used for occasional feast days. Chrysostom preached regularly at the Great/Golden Church. There were also several martyrs' shrines, cemeteries in the suburbs where Chrysostom would preach on martyrs' feast days.[7]

CONSTANTINOPLE

Constantinople was at this time more important than Antioch, both politically—as the capital—and ecclesiastically—as the official center of Eastern Christianity. It was a city of great wealth, the "political, administrative, and cultural center of the Roman Empire, then of the Byzantine Empire."[8] Our best estimates are that the city was between 200,000 and 300,000 people.[9]

To be bishop of Constantinople was thus to be bishop in the capital city of the Eastern Roman Empire. It was to be powerful, considered the unofficial head of the Eastern church.[10] That the emperor and empress were members of Bishop John's congregation helped that designation and

---

6. Mayer, "John Chrysostom," 126–27; Kelly, *Golden Mouth*, 302.

7. Kelly, *Golden Mouth*, 3.

8. Berardino et al., *Encyclopedia of Ancient Christianity*, "Constantinople, city."

9. Kelly, *Golden Mouth*, 107. For a full description of Constantinople in Chrysostom's time, see Kelly, *Golden Mouth*, 107–11.

10. The Council of Constantinople in 381 decreed that after the bishop of Rome, the bishop of Constantinople would have the second place of honor among all bishops. Though there were no official heads yet, Rome and Constantinople had become the capitals and centers of Christianity. The title patriarch of Constantinople as the official head of the Eastern Orthodox Church came about in the sixth century.

gave importance to the city, and these things alone would influence his preaching, at least in some ways.[11]

There was a magnificent horse-racing arena in Constantinople as well, also the target of many of Chrysostom's criticisms in homilies.

Chrysostom's church was the Great Church, though it was probably already beginning to be called Hagia Sophia, the name by which it is now known. There were three other major churches in the city, and though Chrysostom as bishop oversaw of all of them, his work primarily happened at Hagia Sophia.

HISTORICAL MOMENT

There are two especially noteworthy periods of early Christian history that shape the time in which Chrysostom lives: the legalization of Christianity and the Arian controversy or Trinitarian debates. Living after the former gives Chrysostom a political and social context of power that earlier authors did not have, and living after the latter gives Chrysostom a particular theological context.

Prior to the legalization of Christianity in 313 CE, the power dynamics under which Christian authors lived, thought, and wrote were grave. Persecutions were a real threat, though rarely was the persecution empire-wide and state-sponsored. Until the great persecution under Diocletian in 303–6 CE, there were primarily sporadic and localized outbursts of persecution, though these were still horrific. Much Christian writing from that time was in one of two forms. The first form was martyrdom accounts—stories of the martyrs—meant to inspire continued faithfulness

---

11. His biography also makes it clear that he chose not to let it influence him in other ways, assuming as he did that his ecclesiastical authority outranked the imperial authority.

from Christians under threat. Before Christianity was legal, Romans often persecuted Christians and at different periods killed them for being Christians. Those who died because of their faith were called martyrs, and because Christians thought of these people as heroes, they told their stories in order to inspire others who were similarly persecuted.

The second form of writing from this time was defenses of Christianity—called apologies, from the Greek word for defense (*apologia*/ἀπολογία)—written for both Jews and pagans, attempting to show the truth and reasonableness of Christianity in a world that claimed that Christians were subversive, perverted, and dangerous.[12] Though Tertullian notably wrote some systematic and constructive theology that worked to understand the faith more deeply, the focus of most writing of the time was with defense and inspiring followers. Once Christianity became legal, and further once Christianity became the religion of the empire, it became easier to write and so there was more constructive work.

The other reason it is significant that Chrysostom preached after Christianity became legal—in fact, Chrysostom preached after Christianity had become the state religion in 380 CE—is that the relationship between the church and political authority changed. No longer under threat by Roman officials, when Christianity was the religion of the empire, Christianity had the power of the empire and threatened and persecuted non-Christians. The change in power is part of what accounts for the different content and genre of writing, but those writings reflect the reality of the empire, which changes theology. Chrysostom, when bishop

---

12. Perversion was a common charge because rituals like Eucharist/Communion can sound like cannibalism to outsiders, and the act of calling one another "brother" and "sister," even as they marry one another, sounded like incest, among other descriptions and rumors about their rituals. For more on this and other major reasons for persecution, see Gonzalez, *Story of Christianity*, 41–68, 97–104.

of Constantinople, served the imperial church. Christians had actual power, and their theology reflects this, including Chrysostom's.

The second important moment was the Arian controversy or Trinitarian debates. Early in the fourth century, just after Christianity became legal, Christian thinkers were trying to articulate two patterns they saw in Scripture:

1) There is only one God, and
2) Jesus Christ is divine.

Trying to hold both together as true, a priest named Arius suggested that the best interpretation of Scripture is that the Father created the Son at some time before the creation of the world, and the Son is a divine creature who then effected our salvation. Athanasius, another priest (and eventually bishop), was the primary voice against this, arguing that if the Son is a creature—however divine—the Son could not accomplish salvation. His reading of Scripture was that the Father and Son are both eternal, both fully divine, and of the same substance. Emperor Constantine called a council in Nicaea in 325 to insist that the bishops settle what had become a major controversy that threatened to split the church.[13] It was a time of intense theological debate and writing among bishops, but lay people took sides as well. Often lay people from both sides worshiped in the same spaces because for the most part people went to the church closest to them, or the only one in their town. Much of the fervor was faithful people trying to understand who God is when they are receiving different messages, but some was also like people picking a sports team and then entrenching against

13. Gregory of Nyssa famously noted that a person couldn't go to the local bakery without being asked whether they were a *homoiousian* or a *homoousian* (whether the Father and Son were of *similar* or the *same* substance). See *Oratio de deitate Filii et Spiriti Sancti* (*Oration on the Deity of the Son and of the Holy Spirit*) (PG 46:557). There is currently no English translation available.

the other side. Christians were divided in their understanding, and Constantine called them together to figure out the most faithful understanding of God they could. The deliberations of this council led to the formation of the Nicene Creed and what is now the orthodox understanding of a doctrine of the Trinity. There were another fifty-six years of arguments and jockeying, and in 381 bishops held another council in Constantinople where they decreed that the Nicene Creed stood. This was the end of major debate, even as small factions of those who believed other things about the relations among the members of the Trinity still existed.

That Chrysostom writes after the councils of Nicaea and Constantinople means that he is not embroiled in major doctrinal debate. He takes the official line and preaches from there. He does have moments of preaching for orthodoxy and against what has been deemed heresy, and he preaches one twelve-homily series against the Anomeans, a particular group of heretics, but his overall program is about the Christian life rather than Christian doctrine. This emphasis is something that would be different if he were under threat for his life as well as if the doctrinal debates were still raging as debates.

PHILOSOPHY

One aspect of thought impossible to ignore in early Christianity is the influence of Greek philosophy on theology. Since the educational model included philosophy and rhetoric, all of the wealthy young men who grew into theologians were trained in these arts, and it makes sense that the categories of thought and ways of thinking were part of the way they interpreted Scripture and thought about theology. Each theologian is unique in which parts of philosophy he borrows from and how he interacts with it, but it is in the cultural water, and it is helpful to understand what early Christian authors are using, responding to, or challenging if we are to have a good understanding of their thought.

Chrysostom's classical rhetorical training and his homilies themselves reveal that he knew philosophy. Parsing out whose work he knows and which concepts he uses intentionally over against images that are common knowledge or part of the culture is more challenging. When Chrysostom cites a philosopher directly, the task is easy. Over his corpus he cites Zeno, Socrates, Diagoras, Pythagoras, Aristotle, and Plato, whom he mentions thirty times in all.[14]

In these instances of direct quotation or mentioning philosophers by name or as a collection ("the philosophers"), he most often uses them as a foil for Paul or for Christ. Chrysostom talks about how wise they were, or how wise people know them to be, and then says that Christ is wiser than all of them. Or, when he really wants to make a point, that the uneducated fishermen disciples were wiser than Plato himself: "[God] threw out Plato, not through some other wiser philosopher, but through an unlearned fisherman. Thus the defeat became greater and the victory more impressive."[15] Chrysostom is antagonistic, using the philosophers to show the truth and superiority of Christianity. He often states that Christ is the true philosopher and Christianity the true philosophy (*philosohpia*/φιλοσοφία). Ancient philosophers were understood to be teaching a way of life that would lead to wisdom and flourishing, and that way of life was called a philosophy. Chrysostom held that the ancient philosophers' understanding was incomplete, but Christ's way of life was one that led to full and actual

14. *Adv. Jud.* 5.3 (PG 48:886); *Hom. 1 Cor.* 7.7 (PG 61:63); and *Hom. Rom.* 3.2 (PG 60:414). The count of thirty references to Plato is from Baur, *John Chrysostom and His Time*, 1:306.

15. *Hom. 1 Cor.* 4.2 (PG 61:33).

wisdom and flourishing, so Christ was the true philosopher that a person should follow and Christianity was the true way of life to follow to wisdom.

Chrysostom's thought more often, however, shows influence from philosophy through echoes or similar concepts. The primary place we see this is in his teachings on virtue and suffering, which sound similar to Stoic teachings. Stoicism holds that the purpose of human lives is to align one's life with the will of God, which is Nature. In doing so, one will become free of suffering because suffering happens when one resists Nature. Further, Stoic authors highlight the individual's ability to choose, or to make a free choice, as central to what it means to be human. That the choice is free and cannot be coerced in anyway makes a person morally responsible for him- or herself in all situations. Here also the external circumstances of a person's life, even circumstances of suffering, are irrelevant to a person's virtue because the virtue is about the person's free choice. How they respond to external circumstances is the central thing.

Chrysostom's own ideas echo these Stoic concepts. Chrysostom speaks of "true harm" versus "apparent harm" when discussing suffering. Apparent harm is anything external—poverty, disease, even death—and true harm is anything that harms a person's virtue. A fuller description of Chrysostom on virtue and suffering follows in chapter 5; here I only wish to point out that many of these ideas are, if not knowingly, borrowed from Stoicism, or at least influenced indirectly by Stoic ideas. The emphasis on personal moral responsibility because of free choice, the insistence that no one can force a person to make any given choice, the distinction between true and apparent harm, and the dismissal of external life circumstances as irrelevant to virtue are all ideas Chrysostom emphasizes in his own account of human virtue. Chrysostom also explains how Christ's work in incarnation, death, and resurrection are what enable a person to exercise her ability to choose well, which shows that Chrysostom is a Christian rather than a Stoic, even as he uses Stoic ideas.

CHRYSOSTOM'S WRITINGS

As noted in the previous chapter, most of the writing that survives from Chrysostom is his sermons. There are a handful of treatises—pieces on a given topic that he wrote to be circulated—such as his *On Vainglory and the Right Way for Parents to Bring Up Their Children* and his *On Providence*, and we also have some letters that he wrote with Olympias during his exile, but the vast majority of work extant is Chrysostom's homilies.[16]

This means a couple of things both for our understanding of Chrysostom as a theologian and for our ability to understand Chrysostom's thought. First, it means that Chrysostom is not doing speculative theology the way Origen or Gregory of Nyssa were. With one exception, Chrysostom did not write treatises on doctrine or anything one would recognize as systematic theology, attempts to tie all the pieces of his thought into a coherent system.[17] Chrysostom's primary work is the education and moral formation of his congregants, and the way he does this is through

16. For translations see Laistner, *Christianity and Pagan Culture in the Later Roman Empire*; Hall, "John Chrysostom's 'On Providence.'"

17. The exception is his series of homilies *On the Incomprehensible Nature of God* (*De incompr. hom.*), which Chrysostom preaches against the Anomeans (sometimes the series is simply called *Against the Anomeans*) when there is a critical mass of these pro-Arian people in his congregation. Chrysostom preaches to correct the problematic view of the Trinity they circulated. Even here, the medium is a set of homilies rather than a treatise. Chrysostom's focus was the education and protection of his congregation rather than constructive theology. English translation: Harkins, *On the Incomprehensible Nature of God*.

sermons on Scripture, often preaching straight through a book, one homily after another until a book is finished.[18]

Expounding on Scripture as he does, Chrysostom is not doing any kind of constructive theology; he is preaching on whatever topics appear in the Scripture for that day or on whatever topic has occurred to him as connected to the day's biblical text. On occasion he also interrupts a series he is preaching or strays from the day's text in order to address an issue that has happened in the city, such as an earthquake or the riots in Antioch.[19] He is concerned foremost that his people know their basic theology—what Christians believe—and how they should live as Christians, not to develop for them answers to speculative theological questions of the day. As noted above, this is in part due to living after the major decisions at the Councils of Nicaea and Constantinople. Even so, Chrysostom does not partake in the questions surrounding the nature of Christ that had begun by his day and that will reach peak controversy thirty to fifty years after Chrysostom's death.

This also means that Chrysostom's theology is lived rather than speculative. In Chrysostom's time, theology was not siloed off as a discipline for academics. People cared about doctrine because it mattered for how they lived. Chrysostom was not constructing arguments on the finest points of doctrine for the sake of greater abstract knowledge; he expounded on Scripture in order to persuade his congregants to live more faithful and virtuous lives for the sake of their salvation.

---

18. That he is not a speculative theologian led many modern scholars to dismiss Chrysostom as unimportant theologically. Recently scholars have been reevaluating this appraisal and arguing that in fact Chrysostom is doing a lot of sophisticated theology in his homilies. Most pastors know that they are doing theology in the pulpit.

19. See *Laz.* 6.1.

In terms of what the genre of Chrysostom's works means for how we understand Chrysostom's thought, or how we come to understand it, the first aspect is that Chrysostom's theology is spread throughout his homilies rather than located in one place. Because he is preaching the next passage in a book of Scripture, he is attending to what is in front of him. One can see his theology over the course of his corpus, but there is no one homily where he outlines systematically or in detail, for instance, his understanding of salvation or of who Christ is. Readers and scholars must therefore piece together aspects of his thought from many different places in his sermons.

Second, because Chrysostom is not preaching from a pre-written manuscript—today we might say he was preaching extemporaneously—those of us who read Chrysostom have to keep the nature of his homilies in mind. As a rhetorician, he is careful with his words, but since he is preaching without a written manuscript, he is also not measuring each word with the same intentionality he might if he were writing. Therefore, when reading, we have to take his words seriously but not too seriously.

Every preacher knows that she sometimes says something in a particular way in order to make her point, perhaps emphasizing an aspect of an idea that elsewhere she would de-emphasize to make a different point. Or a preacher might use a word that helps get a point across in a sermon that, if analyzed too closely or if made to bear too much weight, might prove to be problematic theology. All of this is to say that Chrysostom was, as a rhetor, choosing his words carefully and intentionally, but his goal was to persuade his audience to believe, think, feel, and live in particular ways. A reader needs to keep that goal in mind as she considers his words—are the choices he made for rhetorical effect or is this revealing a critical piece of his theology, or both? Chrysostom means what he says, and his homilies were and are public, so we can take them as representative of his thought, but it is also important to consider how rhetorical devices and his oratorical aims affect his words.

In the remainder of this book as I outline Chrysostom's thought, I use many sources from across Chrysostom's corpus to construct his understanding of various ideas. Any idea that shows up in multiple places in the same way is likely accurate to Chrysostom's thought. An idea that appears only once, or an interpretation of a statement that is not borne out in other places in Chrysostom's thought, is possibly something he said to make a point in a given sermon but which should not be taken as a central aspect of his thought. I do attend to Chrysostom's word choices, but unless the words appears multiple times in the same way, I do not make word choice the primary load bearer of any argument. It is also important to note that Chrysostom changed over time, including his thought. We see this primarily in his ways of talking about asceticism, but I attend to the chronology of his homilies and any change we see as I can. Chrysostom is fairly consistent throughout his career on most topics, but sometimes changes in wording or ideas can also be attributed to different life circumstances he is experiencing at the time.

That Chrysostom's primary extant works are homilies also means that Chrysostom's aim is to help his audience understand what God is communicating to them through Scripture. He has so much of the Bible memorized that he quotes from Scripture or makes allusions as easily as breathing. Even when he returns to his pet topics—asceticism, virtue, and the like—he does so at the impetus of some pieces of the passage he is explicating. I will talk more specifically about how Chrysostom interprets the Bible in the next chapter. Here I only want to point out that as we investigate Chrysostom's thought, we are doing so through homilies that are first about interpreting Scripture so that his congregation knows how to live. Scripture is the backbone of his thought.

One final note on Chrysostom's homilies: the Bible Chrysostom used would have been very similar to our own. The canon was settled in the late fourth century, about the time Chrysostom was ordained bishop.[20] One significant aspect to note is that Chrysostom was using a version of the Septuagint—the Greek translation of the Hebrew Old Testament—which included what many modern Christians refer to as the Apocrypha or deuterocanonical books. As for most Christians of his time, those books were part of Scripture, and as such, Chrysostom quotes from the Wisdom of Solomon as often as he does from Matthew. In order to get more fully into Chrysostom's mind, one has to remember that the so-called deuterocanonical books are not extraneous but are *part of Scripture* for him. Only then will one see all of the allusions and the full arguments Chrysostom makes.

CONCLUSION

Chrysostom's world was one where the wealthy had extreme wealth—and power—but most people had just enough to get by and some were completely destitute. Furthermore, the poor were not hidden. Chrysostom himself, as bishop in the capital city of the Eastern Roman Empire and priest to the imperial family, had both power (and wealth if he had wanted it) and access to wealth and power, even though he himself sought withdrawal and poverty in keeping with

---

20. Athanasius wrote his Easter letter outlining the books settled as canon in 367, and the Council of Carthage recognized the standard canon in 397 CE, the year Chrysostom was ordained bishop.

the ascetic tradition he believed to be the most faithful way of life, especially for a bishop.

Significantly, Chrysostom lived at a time when Christianity was legal, so he could preach without fear of blanket persecution, and also after the first two major ecumenical councils had met to define the nature of God as Trinity. Because of both of these things, his writing and preaching were able to focus on *living as Christians* rather than explaining or arguing about doctrine.

Like many of his contemporaries, Chrysostom's thought was steeped in philosophy as a result of both his education and his time. His particular fondness appears to be for Stoicism and its understanding of virtue, which Chrysostom furthers in a distinctly Christian way, as he preaches in one homily after another that virtue is the way to live in God's order of the world. That the works we have from Chrysostom are primarily homilies has implications for how we read him and how we understand and make claims about what he thinks and is doing. We must remember Chrysostom's persuasive goal in each individual homily and look at his corpus as a whole to understand his theology rather than at any one standalone comment.

Holding this background context in mind, we turn now to an examination of Chrysostom's thought.

DISCUSSION QUESTIONS

1. What is the impact of Stoicism on Chrysostom's thought, and how does Christian thought carry the philosophy further?
2. What changes does Christianity effect in the ancient world?
3. How are sermons today expressions of theology?

PART 2

CHRYSOSTOM'S THOUGHT

3

PASTORAL THEOLOGY

Chrysostom took his role as priest—and then bishop—seriously. For him, the priest's primary responsibility is to care for the souls in his congregation, which he refers to as caring for the body of Christ and by which he means to care for their salvation. The priest is a spiritual shepherd and spiritual physician. As shepherd he guards congregants from heresy, bad teaching, or any number of the devil's tricks and attacks, and as physician he keeps the body of Christ healthy and whole and heals it when it contracts a disease of some kind. The priest discharges this duty primarily through words, providing people with whatever scriptural and rhetorical remedy their situation calls for. The priest is supposed to persuade his people to believe correctly and live virtuously, which will transform them into Christ-likeness, or into Christians, little Christs. This will finally result in the transformation of the whole city into a Christian city, a heaven on earth. Quite the responsibility, as Chrysostom understands it.

Whatever we can say about his strictness and impassioned rhetoric, about whether he was too controlling or too idealistic, even whether his humility about his own qualifications for the role is more rhetorical than real (an argument but not a certainty), it does appear that Chrysostom was not a priest for the power. His concern does seem to be for his congregants rather than the institution, and not for the power and status he receives from being bishop in the imperial church and having access to the emperor and empress. His concern is that all people live in the virtuous ways that God has ordained and empowered and that resist the devil's destruction. People bring this to the salvation God has wrought for them in Christ and thus live into their own salvation.

ON THE PRIESTHOOD

Chrysostom's explicit pastoral theology is located in his *On the Priesthood*.[1] The work, one of Chrysostom's treatises (rather than sermons), written to his friend Basil, who was upset with Chrysostom for not standing with him when the community wanted to ordain both of them against their wishes, is a defense of Chrysostom's choice to hide from the community and let them ordain Basil alone. In the form of this defense, the piece provides the clearest articulation of Chrysostom's pastoral theology.

According to Chrysostom, he ran from those who would ordain him because the responsibility of the priesthood is enormous and he felt inadequate to meet that responsibility. Ironically, he endorses the idea that those who do not want to be priests are those who should be because those who want to be priests are usually those who should

---

1. John Chrysostom, *Sur le sacerdoce* (ed. Malingrey). For a good English translation, see Neville, *Six Books on the Priesthood*.

Pastoral Theology

not be. Those who want the office, Chrysostom thinks, are those who abuse its power and do not serve for the right reasons. He writes, "Before all other [qualities that a priest must have], he must clear his soul completely from all desire for the office, for if he is overly desirous of that office and he happens to end up in it, then becoming mastered by the desire, he builds the flame stronger and more powerful, enduring myriad evils to keep [his office] secure."[2] Therefore Chrysostom's reluctance is evidence in favor of his own priesthood, though he does not see this for himself. In fact, the majority of Chrysostom's apology is about the responsibility—which he claims he is inadequate to meet—and consequences for failure more than what a priest actually does.

The magnitude of the priest's responsibility and the reason one ought to fear it comes from the nature of that responsibility. Chrysostom explains:

> [Priests] are those—the ones who are trusted
> with spiritual birth pangs and are given charge
> of the birth of baptism. Through them we are
> clothed with Christ and buried with the Son of
> God, becoming limbs of that blessed head.[3]

The range of human life and the very salvation of souls is that for which the priest is responsible. Moreover, priests are the only ones responsible for it. They are the only ones whose task is to protect and facilitate their congregants' salvation, and they will have to give account for them: "How

---

2. *Sac.* 3.10 (SC 172:166–68). Though we can assume some literary necessity in his humility, Chrysostom writes of his response to hearing he will be ordained: "I was seized by fear and embarrassment: fear, that I would be captured some time against my will, and embarrassment, that, seeking often, why it occurred to those men to make such a plan about us. For looking at myself, I couldn't find anything worthy of that honor" (*Sac.* 1.3 [SC 172:72]).

3. *Sac.* 3.5 (SC 172:150).

will we bear [in the world to come], when we are compelled to give an account for each of those who have been entrusted to us? For the penalty is not just disgrace, but eternal punishment waits."[4] For this reason Chrysostom is afraid of the position. He writes, "I am afraid lest, having received the plump and well-fed flock of Christ, then mistreating it through lack of attention, I provoke against myself the God who so loved them that he gave himself for their salvation and honor."[5] Failing in this position is no small matter. To harm the people with whom God entrusted him and for whom God gave himself would be to bring God's wrath on himself.

Accordingly, the consequences for failing this responsibility are grave. It is one thing for a parishioner to be mistaken about theology; it is another for a teacher of doctrine to be mistaken and then teach that theology to a parishioner. The priest is responsible for the education and formation of all his people. If he teaches wrong, he endangers a person's—or many people's—salvation, and that is the worst possible scenario. Chrysostom explains, "One who loses sheep from being carried away by wolves or attacks of robbers or . . . some other accident happening, might meet with some forbearance from the master of the flock. And even if he should demand a judgment, the penalty is only as far as money. But the one entrusted with human beings, the rational flock of Christ, submits to a penalty for the loss of the sheep that is not money but his own soul."[6] If the shepherd loses a sheep because of his own carelessness, poor teaching, or failure to protect, the shepherd pays with his own soul. Later Chrysostom is more specific about the kind of payment this will be: "It is prepared for them to fall into

4. *Sac.* 6.1 (SC 172:304).
5. *Sac.* 2.5 (SC 172:118–20).
6. *Sac.* 2.2 (SC 172:106).

the abyss of fire and death waits—not death that separates the soul from the body but death that escorts into eternal punishment."[7] The one who damages one of Christ's people is thrown into hell's fire and suffers eternal death. With such an understanding of the responsibility, it is a wonder anyone would step forward to be ordained.

PRIEST AS SHEPHERD OR GUARDIAN

As we're seeing, one major metaphor Chrysostom uses for the priest's role is borrowed from Christ and is common language for describing priests in his time. Just as Christ is the Good Shepherd, priests are shepherds of their congregations. The primary aspect of this metaphor on which Chrysostom focuses is protection. Just as a shepherd of sheep guards the lives of the sheep, the priest guards the souls of his congregation from the devil's attempts at destruction. That kind of responsibility requires care and reverence for the work. Yet in contrast to a shepherd of actual sheep, the priest's battle is with more dangerous creatures. Chrysostom writes:

> The fight is not with wolves, nor the fear of robbers.... Against whom is the war?... Listen to St. Paul, who says, "Our struggle is not against flesh and blood, but against the principalities, against powers, against the world rulers of this present darkness, against the spiritual forces of wickedness in the heavenly places." Do you see the terrible multitude and wild phalanx, not defended with iron but whose [evil] nature is enough instead of any armor?[8]

---

7. *Sac.* 3.8 (SC 172:160).
8. *Sac.* 2.3 (SC 172:106–8).

Therefore, because the priest faces attackers more dangerous and more destructive than wolves, and as the priest has such a responsibility to protect the congregation and keep them from error, since the consequences for failure are so grave, the priest needs courage: "Therefore he needs a noble soul in order that he not despair nor neglect the salvation of those who wander, in order that he will continually think and say, 'Perhaps God will give them knowledge of the truth and come to their senses out of the trap of the devil.'"[9] It is not wolves but the devil, intent on humanity's destruction, from whom the priest needs to protect the congregant.

Moreover, this work requires courage and persistence because people's salvation is at stake, and the fight is exhausting. Not only the fight against those who would endanger his congregants but against those who would defame the priest himself. Chrysostom writes:

> It is necessary for the priest to be armed with weapons of steel, both intense earnestness and continual sobriety of life, to keep watch everywhere lest someone discover some naked and neglected place and strike a mortal blow. For everyone stands around prepared to wound and throw him down, not only enemies and foes but many who pretend to love him.[10]

Because of this, the priest needs to be of the highest moral character.

The priest also needs to be wily, cunning, and wise, trained in all the various kinds of tricks the devil will use to attack, so that the devil will find himself blocked at every step, every attempt. The priest is one who does battle with the devil on behalf of his congregants, and he has to not

---

9. *Sac.* 2.4 (SC 172:116).
10. *Sac.* 3.10 (SC 172:182).

only know what kinds of tricks the devil will use but also be accomplished in the tactics that will defeat those tricks. Chrysostom describes the situation:

> This war is varied and waged by different enemies. For they neither use all the same weapons nor have they practiced to attack us in the same way. And it is necessary for anyone who intends to take on the fight to know all the skills. . . . Unless the one who intends to win understands every part of the skill, the devil knows, introducing his minions through one neglected part, to tear apart the flock. But not when the shepherd is aware of all the skill in all areas and beautifully understands his plans.[11]

A good priest is no pushover.

The shepherd-guardian metaphor shows up especially when Chrysostom speaks of the way a priest needs to fend off heresy from his congregants. Chrysostom is concerned both for those who are themselves fighting about heresy as well as those who listen. In *On the Priesthood* Chrysostom lists the dangers of several heresies of the time, such as Marcionism and Arianism, and the kinds of wrong belief the hearing of these ideas can lead innocent parishioners into.[12] We see Chrysostom's fight for orthodoxy in some of his sermons as well, such as his series of homilies against the Anomeans, who argue that God is not Trinity in the way orthodox belief teaches.[13] He has the same protective intent

---

11. *Sac.* 4.3–4 (SC 172:252).

12. For more on Marcionism, Arianism, and the other two heresies Chrysostom names, Sabellianism and Valentinianism, see their entries in Louth, *Oxford Dictionary of the Christian Church*.

13. John Chrysostom, *Sur l'incompréhensibilité de Dieu* (eds. Daniélou et al.). For a good English translation, see Harkins, *On the Incomprehensible Nature of God*.

in his *Against the Jews*, though we want to note that his anti-Semitism there is problematic, something I will discuss at length in chapter 8.[14] Chrysostom also makes comments throughout his biblical homilies about the dangers of a particular heresy or about the importance of a particular doctrine, such as when he interrupts his commentary on Galatians 1 to say that some heretics use verse 1 to say that the Son is lower than the Father, and this is not a proper reading of Scripture.[15] After a paragraph on this tangent, he moves on to verse 2 and continues explicating. This sort of tangent is entirely common in Chrysostom's homilies.

PRIEST AS PHYSICIAN

In addition to the guardian shepherd, the other major metaphor Chrysostom uses to describe the priest's role is physician, and this metaphor shows up all over Chrysostom's work, not only in *On the Priesthood*. Just as a physician holds her patients' physical lives in her hands, so the priest holds his parishioners' spiritual lives—even more valuable, as Chrysostom understands it—in his hands. He explains:

> [Ministry] is about the very body of Jesus. For the Church of Christ is the body of Christ . . . and it is necessary for the one who has been entrusted with it to train it to highest health and irresistible beauty, looking all around everywhere so that there is neither spot nor wrinkle nor any other such disgrace marring its youthful beauty

---

14. Pradels et al., "Bisher vermisste Textstück in Johannes Chrysostomus, Adversus Judaeos, Oratio 2." For an English translation, see Harkins, *Discourses Against Judaizing Christians*. I am following Wendy Mayer's assessment that the title is *Against the Jews* rather than *Against the Judaizers*, as it has often been translated. Her argument is persuasive in her Mayer, "Preaching Hatred?"

15. *Hom. Gal.* 1.3 (PG 61:616).

and lovely appearance. For what else is there, but to make it worthy, as far as is within human power, of his pure and blessed head which it is under.[16]

This is no easy task. Chrysostom exclaims, "How can [priests] keep [the body of Christ] pure and healthy, unless they have exceptional—beyond human capacity—virtue and thoroughly understand every useful therapy for the soul?"[17] As difficult as it is to keep a physical body healthy, it is more challenging to keep Christ's body healthy because it is more susceptible to disease and the kinds of diseases it acquires require more skill to treat and more time to heal. The priest needs more wisdom and more patience than a physician.

The primary role of the priest physician is to provide the parishioner—the patient—with the particular "dose" of Scripture and rhetoric that she needs at that moment. It could be that the person needs encouragement for something, but she might need rebuke instead. Perhaps she needs a lesson in doctrine or a bit of fear. The priest's job is to attend to each person, recognize the symptoms and the disease, know the appropriate treatment (what the person needs in his given situation), and apply that particular remedy.[18] Chrysostom writes, "There is one skill [a priest] gives

16. *Sac.* 4.2 (SC 172:248).
17. *Sac.* 4.2 (SC 172:248).
18. Chrysostom writes, "He must be many-sided. . . . [N]ot a charlatan, a flatterer, or a hypocrite, but fully free and bold in speech, knowing how to accommodate usefully when the situation demands and to be similarly kind or severe. For it is not profitable to be one way with everyone all the time, just as it is not good for doctors to apply one remedy to all illnesses. . . . Both great accommodation and great strictness are needed. And all of these different remedies are so that we might see one goal: the glory of God and the building up of the Church" (*Sac.* 6.4 [SC 172:320]).

for the work and one way of therapy: the teaching of the word. This is the best tool, the best food, the best climate; it is in place of medicine, cautery, and surgery."[19] Teaching is the primary medicine available to the priest, and the priest needs to be accomplished in all of its arts so that he knows what kind of teaching to apply when.[20]

The reason rhetoric is the preacher's primary tool is rooted in Chrysostom's commitment to moral responsibility.[21] Chrysostom writes:

> It is necessary to make by persuading him thus, not by forcing him. For the authority to check sinners has not been given to us by the law, nor, if it had been, would we know how to use it, since those who are crowned by God are kept from evil not by force but by choice.[22]

Because every person is free and able to choose, every person is responsible for his or her choices. Therefore a priest cannot compel others—was not given by God any means of compelling—or else those people would not be responsible for their choices and would be ineligible for the great rewards at the last judgment. Thus a priest must rely on persuasion.

Since rhetoric and persuasion are the priest's instruments, Chrysostom says that the priest needs to be

---

19. *Sac.* 4.3 (SC 172:250).

20. Sacraments were also the main job of the priest and understood to be a kind of medicine by Chrysostom and his contemporaries, but since those are given and received at standard times as part of worship, Chrysostom focuses on the preaching work of the priest in this treatise, as it is the work the priest can be skilled in.

21. I discuss Chrysostom's account of responsibility, freedom, and virtue in detail in chapter 5.

22. *Sac.* 2.3 (SC 172:112).

Pastoral Theology

spectacularly eloquent and also unaffected by people's opinions.[23] If one is to say harsh things, one has to be eloquent so there is no excuse for those who do not want to be corrected to dismiss his words or attack the priest's ability. Chrysostom writes:

> When he stands in the congregation saying things able to rouse those living lazily, then he stumbles and breaks his speech, and he is forced to blush because of his deficiency, the profit from what he has said leaks away directly. For those who have been censured, suffering from what he said and not being able to defend themselves in another way, throw jeers of stupidity at him, supposing to cover their disgrace by this.[24]

Chrysostom follows up on this and says further that the priest needs this disposition if he is going to be able "to punish or pardon all those who are assigned to him."[25] This language suggests the priest is not only physician but parent as well. Chrysostom then says as much: "The priest needs to minister to those he rules as a father ministers to very young children. Just as we are not turned by their insults or blows or wailing, nor by their laughter and joy toward us."[26] So the priest needs to be skilled at reading people, at rhetoric, at discerning needs, and also to be of the highest moral character, unaffected by others' words or thoughts about him.

In order to do this work well, the priest must have a peculiar kind of knowledge and experience: "It is necessary for [a priest] to be not only pure . . . but also very wise and experienced in many things. He needs to know all things

23. *Sac.* 5.2 (SC 172:286).
24. *Sac.* 5.3 (SC 172:286).
25. *Sac.* 5.3 (SC 172:286).
26. *Sac.* 5.4 (SC 172:288).

about life as those who live in the middle of them but wish to be delivered from them more than the monks who have gone to the mountains."[27] Chrysostom is describing the life of a monk for one who lives in the city. I will show in the next chapter that this is often how Chrysostom describes the ideal Christian who is not a monk. The priest needs to understand all matters of daily life that his parishioners experience but be entirely detached from them so that he is not drawn in and affected. Being able to hold experiences of the world loosely allows the priest to be impartial and provide wisdom and remedies to his congregants, but he will not know what the issues are if he does not know the realities of life in the city.

The knowledge is not rhetoric and worldly affairs alone, either. Yes, someone might need chastisement for an act they did, but in order to bring about repentance, the person might need an example or an imperative from Scripture. Chrysostom often uses stories from the Bible as examples of what his congregants should do, think, feel (or not do, think, or feel). When he discusses resistance to demons or how to suffer well, he tells his congregants that Job ought to be their example. He suffered virtuously and shows others what is possible.[28] Cain is an example of what happens when a person allows jealousy and rage to overtake them. Most often, though, Paul is Chrysostom's example of the ideal Christian.[29] Chrysostom holds up Paul as an example of most virtues for Christians to imitate as they attempt to live virtuously in imitation of God. The priest needs to know the Scripture well enough to pick out

27. *Sac.* 6.4 (SC 172:318).

28. *Diab.* 2.7.

29. For more on Chrysostom's elaborate use of Paul as exemplar and his use of exemplar portraits in the tradition of classic rhetoric, see Mitchell, *Heavenly Trumpet*.

which part to apply to a given scenario. Together the skillfully used Scripture and rhetoric can prick the conscience to repentance or goad the fainthearted to courage or pull a person up short who needs to show some fear and caution.

PREACHING AS PHILOSOPHICAL THERAPY

This aspect of Chrysostom's preaching goes back to Chrysostom's idea that rhetoric is the remedy for spiritual ills (dispensed by the priest, the spiritual physician), and it is not new with Chrysostom. In fact, he understands himself to be a physician in the line of the philosophical physicians who use rhetoric to persuade and shape their hearers' lives, going so far as to say they are healing sick souls.[30] They are doing therapy—in a physical medical, rather than mental health, sense—with rhetoric.[31] Through rhetoric they can manage wayward emotions, which are caused by false reasoning and which are tied in this ancient understanding to morality. A moral soul is a well-ordered soul (ordered by reason), and an immoral or sick soul is a disordered soul. Rhetoric is the medicine that can re-order a soul properly, managing the emotions and putting everything in its place. Once everything is in its proper place, the person will live virtuously. Chrysostom tells his congregants:

> We send this disease packing. How and by what means? By preparing the medicine of rhetoric.
> . . . This treatment nourishes more than bread,

30. There has been a lot of research activity recently on Chrysostom's medical-philosophical approach to his work, noting the techniques Chrysostom favors. See Mayer, "Persistence in Late Antiquity of Medico-Philosophical Psychic Therapy"; Mayer, "Shaping the Sick Soul."

31. Ancient philosophers understood rhetoric to be a kind of therapy or medical treatment for the soul. For more on this, see the resources listed in the previous footnote.

> restores more effectively than a drug and cauterizes more powerfully than fire without causing any pain. At the same time it checks the foul-smelling discharges of perverse reasonings. Sharper than iron, it painlessly cuts away the infected areas.[32]

The priest uses rhetoric to persuade a person's reason into believing the right things, and when the person's reason is in order, they will be able to put their emotions in order and live well.

One aspect of this work is the way Chrysostom uses emotion in his preaching to persuade his listeners to change their minds and thus their behavior.[33] He uses words and scriptural examples in order to provoke particular strong emotions in his hearers that can be the impetus for change. He even tells parents to use this kind of method when teaching their children. For instance, fear can be a great motivator. Chrysostom preaches vivid descriptions of hell and tells his audience that they will not want to experience the unceasing pain of hell and therefore should change their behavior now so that they will not have to endure hell when they die. This passage is representative:

> The Kingdom urges the good, and hell frightens usefully. For God threatens hell, not in order to throw into hell, but in order that he may set free from hell. If he wanted to punish, he would not threaten ahead of time that we might safely flee the things he threatens. He threatens

---

32. *Scand.* Prol.2.1 (SC 79:52–60). Translation in Mayer, "Persistence in Late Antiquity of Medico-Philosophical Psychic Therapy," borrowing from Hall, "John Chrysostom's 'On Providence.'"

33. For a thorough treatment of Chrysostom's use of emotions, see Leyerle, *Narrative Shape of Emotion*. For more specific case studies, see Moore, "Bound Together"; Papadogiannakis, "Homiletics and the History of Emotions."

punishment so that we might flee the experience of punishment. He frightens with words so that he will not punish with actions.[34]

For Chrysostom, hell is useful.[35]

Elsewhere Chrysostom provides guidance about proper forms of grief and anger, using reason and rhetoric to persuade his congregants that rage makes them look foolish or that grief over losing possessions shows misplaced priorities. He also occasionally provokes grief, anger, and fear with the hope of goading his congregants out of their laziness and into virtuous living. As he understands it, the primary sin is laziness or listlessness. When a person is lazy, he is not vigilant against temptations to sin and more easily gives into sin, damaging his virtue. Chrysostom tries to provoke strong emotions through his preaching in order to shake the lethargy out of his congregants and rouse them to vigilance and resistance.[36] Such work with emotions requires great skill with words: knowing the right words to use, knowing the right emotion that is awry or that needs provoking, knowing which kinds of words will achieve the goal, knowing which scriptural example will serve the argument and finally persuade the congregant to live more virtuously. For Chrysostom, the skill required for the therapy of souls is greater than the skill required for therapy of the body.

---

34. *Paenit.* 7.7 (PG 49:336).

35. For an exploration of Chrysostom's use of hell in his preaching, see my Miller, "Hellish Homiletic Practices."

36. For more on this argument, see Leyerle, *Narrative Shape of Emotion*, 150–82.

TRANSFORMATION OF THE CITY

Even therapy of the soul is not an individual enterprise, though. Chrysostom's overall goal is to transform his hearers into Christians who live like Christians so that the city will itself be transformed into a Christian city, a heaven on earth.[37] In his understanding, God's work is to renew earth into the heaven it was intended to be, and as much as human beings live virtuous Christian lives, they establish heavenly cities on earth and participate in the transformation God is working.

Thus the priest's responsibility is not only to his individual congregants but to the city.[38] As I noted in chapter 2, Chrysostom is living in an empire that considers itself Christian, and when he is bishop in Constantinople the emperor and empress are in his congregation, so there is a different sense to "responsibility to the city" than there is now in North America, but he does understand his role to be about directing the city to act and therefore be properly Christian. This is the root of his strife with the emperor and empress: Chrysostom assumes his pastoral authority is greater than imperial authority as he works toward God's transformation of the world, and the rulers assume their imperial authority is greater than Chrysostom's pastoral authority. Chrysostom takes responsibility for the salvation of the city, not only that of individuals.

One way we see this play out is in the other duties of the priest that Chrysostom names in *On the Priesthood* and that he carries out. Though the vast majority of *On the Priesthood* is the description of what a difficult and dangerous role and responsibility the priest has in preaching, there is

---

37. For more on this theme in Chrysostom, see Hartney, *John Chrysostom and the Transformation of the City*; and Mitchell, "John Chrysostom."

38. Ang, "Examining John Chrysostom's Ideal of the Ascetic Priest," 349–61.

a small section toward the end where Chrysostom enumerates the non-preaching duties of the priest and how those can be challenging in different ways. He lists ministry to the widows, which was primarily about making sure the church was supporting the widows financially; doing pastoral care with widows, or, as he says it, being able to bear with them, because old women tend to fuss and complain; provide hospitality to strangers and care for the sick in the community; care and administration of the nuns; judging disputes between parishioners; visiting parishioners as well as other priests and bishops; and, when needed, excommunicating wayward members who refuse to repent.[39] In all of these duties the priest is working to maintain a Christian city.[40]

CONCLUSION

John Chrysostom's pastoral theology can be summed up as a ministry of protective and healing words. The priest is a shepherd who cares for Christ's sheep and protects them from heresy and from the destructive aims of the devil. The priest is also a spiritual physician whose job is to diagnose any ailment that endangers a person's salvation and then treat the ailment with the appropriate dose of rhetoric—encouragement, rebuke, scriptural example, fear, correction of heresy. Though that can be in personal pastoral conversations, the priest most often discharges this duty in the pulpit, in his preaching. Through preaching he persuades his listeners to live more virtuously so as to participate in their salvation and transform the city into a heavenly city.

---

39. *Sac.* 3.12–14 (SC 172:200–224).

40. We will see in the next chapter that Chrysostom believes *all* Christians, not only the rulers, need to contribute to the transformation of the city into a Christian city. Therefore the priest is working with all people, not only the powerful, to enact this transformation.

PART 2: CHRYSOSTOM'S THOUGHT

DISCUSSION QUESTIONS

1. What do you think of Chrysostom's general principle that people who want to become priests should not? What are the implications for the role of the community when it comes to ministry?
2. Why do you suppose St. Paul (and not Jesus) is held up by John as an example so frequently?
3. Chrysostom notes that those who are not eloquent should not become priests. Why is rhetoric the priest's most important tool?

4

ASCETICISM

When Chrysostom was a young man and a newly baptized Christian, he threw himself into the ascetic life. For him, as for many of his time, monks were the truest Christians, and so Chrysostom, who was an intense person anyway, wanted to be an extreme ascetic and pursue the Christian life to the fullest. When his asceticism proved too extreme for his body to handle, he capitulated to its—in his understanding—weakness, came down from the mountains back to the city, and submitted to ordination. His high regard for asceticism continued, however, and became a major theme of Chrysostom's preaching and writing.

WHAT ASCETICISM IS

First, a definition. The word "asceticism" comes from the Greek *askesis* (ἄσκησις), which means a training regimen or exercise. Originally an athletic term, Christians used it to refer to the spiritual exercises they did to train their souls to contemplate God: prayer, fasting, Scripture reading, keeping vigils, and so on. It became a term to refer to those who went out to the desert or mountains to live apart from society in their pursuit of God because of the practices they undertook and because they were understood to be athletes of God.

The things ascetics understood themselves to be fighting were their passions, or bad thoughts. Though in English "passion" means an extremely strong emotion, the ancient Greeks understood "passion" (*pathos*/πάθος) to be a technical term. Passions in this sense are the over-attachments people have to things other than God, which take them away from God: lust, gluttony, greed, pride, etc. By fasting, a person learns to have a proper relationship with food and therefore combats gluttony; celibacy combats and controls lust, leading to a proper relationship with human love. The goal of asceticism was *apatheia* (ἀπάθεια), a life without those passions. A better way to say it in modern English is an imperturbability even during the chaos of life. That meant their primary attachment was to God and they could live in friendship with God without being distracted by things to which they were overly attached. In short, they were trying to rid themselves of distractions so that their attention could be always on God and they could "pray without ceasing."[1]

The other name for ascetics, those people who went away from the cities to live a life focused on asceticism in order to live a life focused on God, is monks. This was the life Chrysostom wanted to live, did live for a while, and then continually exhorted his congregants to live.

---

1. 1 Thess 5:17.

MONKS ARE THE BEST!

Chrysostom never gives up the idea that asceticism is the best way of life or that the monks are those living the most faithful lives. He even encourages his congregants to adopt and adapt the monks' ascetic way of life for their own lives in the city. Two of Chrysostom's earliest writings are *Comparison Between a King and a Monk* and a set of three homilies *Against the Opponents of the Monastic Life*.[2] The topic of both pieces is to show how the monks' way of life is superior to all other ways of living. Two of the homilies are addressed to parents of young men who want to become monks against their parents' wishes. Chrysostom writes that such parents should be proud, not ashamed, of their children's desire to become monks, for the monk's life is so much better than that of the best politicians, even that of the king himself.

What makes the ascetic life so much superior for Chrysostom? It is more stable, is less dangerous, and receives an ultimate and more important glory. Whereas the king and other wealthy men fear losing their wealth all the time and so are perpetually anxious, the monk has no possessions, lives simply, and therefore has nothing to steal. He does not worry because he does not have any possessions to worry about. To parents worried about their children's reputations, Chrysostom says it is not going away to be a monk that will ruin their reputation. On the contrary, whereas there are all kinds of ways for a young man to ruin his reputation in the city, in the mountains he will have no such opportunities. Chrysostom writes that the monk is free from "madness and turmoil" and does not "lust with

2. *Comparatio regis et monachi* (*Comp. reg. mon.*), PG 47:387–92; *Adversus oppugnatores vitae monasticae* (*Oppugn.*), PG 47:319–86. English translation of both: Hunter, *Comparison and Against the Opponents*.

an insatiable lust."³ He asks pagan parents: "If it were possible . . . to be free of the evils which come from wealth, would you not choose this . . . so as not to suffer jealousy, slander, cares?"⁴ Then he writes, "Avarice will be conquered more easily, not by the person who is caught in the midst of worldly activity, but by the one who lives in the mountains."⁵ Even the monks' sleep is better than a king's:

> If we wished also to examine the nighttime, we would see the monk . . . living with the angels, conversing with God, enjoying the goods of heaven. But he who commands many nations and peoples and armies, who rules over much land and sea, him you will see stretched out on a couch snoring.⁶

In every way, the monk's life is superior to what most people assume is the prestigious life.

Chrysostom wrote both of those pieces early (*Comp. reg. mon.* ca. 368–72; *Oppugn.* ca. 379–83) either while a monk himself or during his period of wanting to go out and live the solitary life but unwilling to do so against his mother's wishes. That is to say, Chrysostom wrote both of these while consumed with fervor for the monastic life. His resolve about the prominence of asceticism continues throughout his career, though.⁷ When the monks came

---

3. *Oppugn.* 2.3 (PG 47:335; Hunter, *Against*, 100).
4. *Oppugn.* 2.3 (PG 47:335–36; Hunter, *Against*, 100–101).
5. *Oppugn.* 3.15 (PG 47:375; Hunter, *Against*, 160–61).
6. *Comp. reg. mon.* 3 (PG 47:389; Hunter, *Comparison*, 72).

7. Wendy Mayer argues that Palladius's account of this continued monasticism was not idealized and possibly presenting an Egyptian, rather than Syrian, version of asceticism, and Chrysostom was not as much a monk as he wants us to believe once he became bishop. See Mayer, "What Does It Mean to Say That John Chrysostom Was a Monk?"

down from their mountain caves and into Antioch to intercede with the emperor on behalf of the city, Chrysostom talks about the monks this way: "Even though [the monks] had been shut up in their cells for so many years, . . . when they saw such a cloud surrounding the city, they left their tents and caves . . . as if they had been so many angels coming to our aid from heaven."[8] He speaks about the life of the monks as heavenly: "For their dwellings are in a state in no way inferior to the heavens, for the angels and the Lord of the angels dwell with them."[9] The monks' life is so good that it is not even inferior to heaven.

We also see Chrysostom's commitment to the ascetic life in Palladius's account of Chrysostom's career. Many of the reforms Chrysostom made and attempted to make were about clergy and bishops living less luxuriously. Chrysostom famously—according to Palladius—angered both political and church officials because he refused to eat with them as a result of his own fasting.[10] Mostly, though, it is Chrysostom's insistence throughout his career—and even through the letters he writes as he is dying to his friend Olympias—that everyone should be like the monks that tells us that he still thinks the ascetic life is the best way of life.

IMITATE THE MONKS!

Because monks have the best way of life, Chrysostom often tells his people to imitate the monks. When he is young and just back to the city from ascetic life himself, Chrysostom means that everyone should go out and become ascetics in

---

8. *Stat.* 17.1 (PG 49:172–73).

9. *Hom. Matt.* 69.3 (PG 58:653). For more on how Chrysostom thinks monks are exemplars of the Christian life, see Lai, "Monk as Christian Saint and Exemplar in St John Chrysostom's Writings."

10. For fuller discussion of this practice, see n.20 on page 19.

the wilderness. In his earliest treatise, he says that monks are like people running out of a burning building and telling others to flee as well. Chrysostom wishes people could "accomplish the virtuous deeds needed to avoid punishment [hell]" at home, in the cities, but he thinks it is not possible in this time. People must flee to the desert or the mountains to do this because the cities "are filled with much lawlessness and injustice, whereas the desert blossoms with the abundant fruit of philosophy."[11] In his early zeal for the ascetic life he characterizes the city as a place so unjust and depraved that no one could possibly reach acceptable virtue while living there; they have to imitate the monks by leaving the city and living ascetic lives in the desert where they can be free of the distractions and not tempted by the lawlessness.

Later, however, as Chrysostom takes up the priesthood and the pulpit, he starts to suggest that Christians in the cities can imitate the ascetic tendencies and virtues of the monks right where they are, without going to the desert. Chrysostom begins to say that it is the detachment—the *apatheia* goal of ascetic practice—that is vital for virtue, not the location or the act of withdrawal itself. Chrysostom preaches, "Come to me, and I will show you the dwellings of these holy ones; come and learn something useful from them. . . . For this reason they lived in solitude, that they might teach you to despise the clamor in the midst of the world."[12] Wherever they are, whatever form of life they have, people can and should live like monks, since monks have a way of life that is an example of the calm imperturbability that allows for contemplation of God. Monks "despise the clamor" of the world by going away from it. City Christians can also learn from the monks how to "despise the clamor" even while they live in the midst of the world.

11. *Oppugn.* 1.7 (PG 47:328; Hunter, *Against*, 90).
12. *Hom. Matt.* 72.4 (PG 58:672).

Asceticism

This detachment from worldly things for the purposes of attachment to God is what Chrysostom wants people to learn from the monks. They can find a calm center even amid all the distractions and concerns of surviving in the world: family, work, all manner of responsibilities. Though, he concedes, it might be slightly more difficult for city folk to do than for the monks because monks are not married and because there are fewer distractions in the desert than in the city.[13] In all other ways, Chrysostom says people in the cities can live just as well as the monks, no excuses. They can see the monks' detachment in stark physical ways and imitate it internally. They can be married but not hold their spouse too tightly, knowing that God is the most important relationship. They can have jobs but hold the job loosely and trust only in God for security. They can earn money but still give most of it away to the poor.

Chrysostom goes further to insist that not only *can* all people reach this state of detachment and contemplation, but they are *expected* to. He writes, "All people must reach the same point! And this is what overturns the whole world, the idea that only the monk is required to show a greater perfection, while the rest are allowed to live in laxity. But this is not true! It is not! Rather, he [Paul] says, the same philosophy is demanded of all."[14] Unlike some of his contemporaries, for Chrysostom, the monks are not somehow super-Christians, not somehow intrinsically more holy. For him, they are living the life of full attention to God, but that only makes them an example. A life oriented entirely to

---

13. "If, therefore, he can be saved with a city and a house and a wife, how much more is this possible without these things!" (*Oppugn.* 3.13 [PG 47:372]).

14. *Oppugn.* 3.14 (PG 47:374; Hunter, *Against*, 158). "Philosophy" for Chrysostom indicates the Christian life.

God where one's passions and thoughts are controlled is the expectation for all Christians regardless of where they live.

In fact, Chrysostom says, if a city-dwelling Christian can manage contemplation and imperturbability, they are even holier because it is harder for them than for the monks. He tells them:

> [The monks] do not need the help of the divine Scriptures as much as those who are twisted up in the middle of many affairs.... They are settled far from the battle; therefore they do not receive many wounds. But you [the city-dwelling congregants] constantly stand in the front of the battle, and you constantly receive blows.[15]

The life of detachment was easier for monks than city-dwellers primarily because city-dwellers would be married and have jobs. With marriage, children, and daily work come more distractions from an unceasing focus on God. Married people and parents are concerned for one another's welfare and the welfare of their children. They are concerned about their children's reputations, about illness and hunger, about providing for the family. They worry that a spouse or child might die. If they do die, the person is full of grief, another distraction from contemplating God. In this way, those in the cities have more concerns and have to work harder against tempting and more present distractions in the battle for contemplation, which is the goal of Christian life.

Chrysostom does not seem to think that a married person in the city will spend every second contemplating God—the person will need to meet the basic needs of his life and his family's lives—but Chrysostom does think that people in cities, even while living in the midst of worldly distractions,

---

15. *Laz.* 3.1 (PG 48:992).

can live lives of detachment. They can hold their worldly distractions loosely and in proper relationship to God.

WHY TO IMITATE: THE ANGELIC LIFE

The question is why Chrysostom insists that everyone should imitate the monks, why he believes that asceticism is the best way to be a Christian. For Chrysostom, asceticism is not only the practices that lead to contemplation of God, it is the angelic life, the life of heaven lived now on earth. I will explore the relationship of this to his idea of salvation in chapter 7, but here it is important to say that the reason asceticism is so important, the reason that the monks who live it are examples, is that a life of perpetual contemplation of God is the life of heaven. Asceticism leads to living now the way Christians will live in heaven, in genuine friendship and closeness with God.

Chrysostom often says that monks are living this angelic life, or the heavenly life. The "angelic life" was a common descriptor of monastic life during Chrysostom's time, drawing from Jesus' saying that in the life to come people will be like the angels, who neither marry nor are given in marriage.[16] Thus, those who choose a celibate life are like the angels. The descriptor grew to include all aspects of the monastic life, but celibacy was still the primary distinguishing mark of the monk over against Christians in the city, and so for Chrysostom and his contemporaries, monks were referred to as angels or as living an angelic life. What makes Chrysostom different from those around him was his insistence that *all* Christians, regardless of their position in life, could become angels.

More than just the idea that an ascetic, angelic life is living the heavenly life before one's earthly life has ended,

16. Matt 22:23–34; Mark 12:18–27; Luke 20:27–40.

getting more of the joy and reward of living in close relationship with God now and not having to wait, Chrysostom insists on asceticism and living the angelic life now because it was the life human beings were intended to live from their creation. The people other than monks that Chrysostom primarily refers to as living "angelic lives" or "heavenly lives" are Adam and Eve before their fall. Chrysostom preaches, "Just like some angel, this is how the human passed his time on earth, wearing a body, but happening to be free of bodily needs; . . . he reveled in living in freedom and great affluence in paradise."[17] Adam and Eve experienced freedom from bodily necessity, just like the angels, who Chrysostom seems to say have no bodies, or at least not material ones like human beings.[18]

This angelic life and its detachment and imperturbability (*apatheia*) is what humanity forfeited when they chose to disobey God in the garden. Chrysostom preaches, "From then on [after the fall] [God] made them dependent on their bodily necessities, depriving them of the angelic way of life and its *apatheia*."[19] Now human beings are aware of their bodies' needs, subject to bodily necessities and limits, and perturbed by the struggles of this life, including labor and sweat, more struggle that is not itself a life of *apatheia*. Describing the thing humanity had at their creation, the thing they then lost, and the thing they are trying to reach again as *apatheia* suggests that, for Chrysostom, the "*apatheia* of the angels" is not merely a reward for living an

17. *Hom. Gen.* 13.3 (PG 53:109).

18. Chrysostom does not talk about this in any systematic way but does make the distinction that humans have bodies and angels do not. For an interesting counter idea, see G. Smith, "How Thin Is a Demon?" Many ancients seemed to think that demons had immaterial bodies, and since angels and demons are the same creations ontologically, it follows that angels would have the same immaterial bodies.

19. *Hom. Gen.* 18.2 (PG 53:150).

ascetic life, not merely a pleasant and easier earthly existence, not merely the goal of human life, but the very form of salvation. This is what Christians ought to be aiming at and why they practice asceticism. It will lead to a return to life they were created for.

In one homily Chrysostom asks his audience to consider which of two hypothetical people is more virtuous: someone who amasses as much gold as he can, or one who gives to the poor, heals the sick, frees those in the mines, and so on. He concludes the section, "Is not the one person like some angel who has come down from heaven for the restoration of the rest of humanity?"[20] This most virtuous person is not a monk he is describing but someone who lives and works in the city, who is probably married. Giving to the poor, healing people, freeing people: these are practices that lead to being like the angels, just like he describes the monks. Here he suggests that Christians in the cities can also become like angels by their virtue. It is not even about the ascetic life, except implicitly, as denying oneself possessions or comforts is how one would be so devoted to caring for the people around one. Asceticism is not the goal, but neither is virtue, as we will see in the following chapter. Asceticism and virtue *lead to* an angelic life. Then Chrysostom goes on to pose another hypothetical: "Which one is excellent, tell me: the one who is puffed up and inflamed, or the one who is self-restrained? Is it not again the one who is like the powers from above who have so much *apatheia*?"[21] The virtuous person is one who cares for the people around him and is self-restrained, and these things make him like the angels who have *apatheia*, that imperturbable calm because they are attached solely to God and not distracted or thrown off by the struggles of life.

20. *Hom. Matt.* 23.9 (PG 57:320).
21. *Hom. Matt.* 23.10 (PG 57:320).

PART 2: CHRYSOSTOM'S THOUGHT

Chrysostom spends more time telling his people to live ascetic lives in the cities than he does describing what that city asceticism ought to look like, but he does offer occasional comments on the topic. The thing he says most often is that people should turn their homes into little monasteries. The father, as the head of the household, should be the abbot and love and guide his wife and children. He should lead them in reading Scripture together as a family, they should discuss the day's homilies together after worship, and they should pray together. Chrysostom preaches:

> When you leave here, set a spiritual table too. And let the father speak about something that was said here. Let his wife hear, and let the children learn from it, and let even the servants be taught. Then let the house become a church in order that the devil be driven off and that evil spirit, the enemy of our salvation, runs off. The grace of the Holy Spirit would rest upon it instead and all peace and harmony would surround those who live there.[22]

It is a lofty goal. Notice that Chrysostom says the order of a home as church reflects the order of a monastery, which is peace and harmony, which is the order of heaven. Chrysostom imagines that each family head orders himself with asceticism, then orders his home, and when all homes order themselves, the city is ordered, and all together mirror the order of heaven.[23]

The other main thing that Chrysostom describes as practice for those in cities is almsgiving. I'll go more in depth on this in chapter 6, but here I want to note that almsgiving is, in part, an ascetic practice for Chrysostom.

22. *Hom. Gen.* 2.4 (PG 53:31).

23. Once he even said he wished the whole city would become like a monastery. *Hom. Rom.* 26.4 (PG 60:644).

Wealth is a distraction from God, so giving alms removes a distraction and makes it easier to focus on God. Chrysostom even speaks of the family "church" as an almsgiving institution: "Make your house a church, your alms-box a treasury. Become a protector of holy money, a self-appointed manager of the poor. Your philanthropy gives you this priesthood."[24] Together these practices allow city-dwelling Christians to live the angelic life of imperturbable calm in the midst of the clamor of their world.

CONCLUSION

Chrysostom's commitment to asceticism was lifelong. Forced to return from his own time as a monk when his health failed, ordained, and then eventually made bishop, he did not himself live the ascetic life he wanted to live when he was young, though according to his biographers he did attempt to keep a kind of asceticism in his way of life and leading as bishop. For Chrysostom, as for many of his time, monks were the truest Christians, living most fully in line with God's desires for humanity. Their detachment from the things of the world facilitated their attachment to and contemplation of God, setting them apart.

Chrysostom, however, insisted to his congregants that they too could live like the monks, and they should. People ought to imitate the monks where they were in the cities, married and all. In that way, everyone could live the angelic existence God had intended for humanity from the beginning. Human beings forfeited their angelic way of being with God in the garden when they sinned, but Chrysostom said that living ascetic practices, even among the distractions of daily city life, could lead to the *apatheia* Adam and Eve enjoyed before the fall. They could even reach a communion

24. *Hom. 1 Cor.* 43.1 (PG 61:368–69).

with God. Then, if everyone did this, the city could be an outpost of heaven here on earth. That, he believed, was the goal.

DISCUSSION QUESTIONS

1. Why might monasticism be seen as the highest ideal of the Christian life?
2. What is the role of asceticism in the Christian life? How might it be lived out today?

5

VIRTUE, OR THE CHRISTIAN LIFE

As a priest and as a bishop, Chrysostom's primary concern was for his people's present and future life with God. His encouragement to his people to live virtuously was relentless. As I noted, his sermons walked through scriptural texts one passage at a time until he finished a book, but within these homilies—often an hour or more long—virtue and the way his congregants live were a primary theme. Nearly every sermon ended with an exhortation to a particular way of living or a call to live virtuously.

This emphasis is so prominent that for much of modern Christian history people have ignored Chrysostom because they say he is "just a moralist."[1] He is uninteresting

---

1. I mean in the last couple of hundred years since scholars have focused so much on systematic theology and development of doctrine rather than piety and living. In the Enlightenment, ways of thinking in the Western world became more focused on rationality and provability, and theology similarly divided further into abstract

or does not have a sophisticated theology because he is a preacher, or he is not saying anything unique enough among his contemporaries to be worth listening to today. That assessment has been changing in the last fifty years as a number of scholars have been looking more intently at Chrysostom's work and discussing his theology and his overall program as a preacher.[2] After all, if we dismiss preachers as theologians, we dismiss the majority of theology being done in the world at all times and in all places. Scholarly conversation aside, it is easy to see why people gave Chrysostom the designation "moralist." He preaches about virtue and the Christian life at every turn.

VISION OF THE CHRISTIAN LIFE

Let me start with Chrysostom's overall image of the Christian life. The place he describes this most explicitly is in his baptismal homilies.[3] Chrysostom preached a series of twelve sermons to the people about to be baptized that year. Three homilies were preached in the days leading up to their baptism, one the night of their baptism at the Easter Vigil, and eight in the days immediately after their baptism. As now, baptism was the sacrament that signaled a person's entrance into the church. Different from now, the requirements for baptism and the responsibilities and restrictions associated with baptism were much more rigorous. Non-baptized members of the congregation would be dismissed

---

doctrine over against devotional or lived work. The priority of reason led scholars to elevate systematic theology as more sophisticated and therefore more worthy of exploration than homilies or other work aimed at moral living for Christians.

2. For a start on this reassessment, see Rylaarsdam, *John Chrysostom on Divine Pedagogy*; De Wet and Mayer, *Revisioning John Chrysostom*.

3. Critical edition: John Chrysostom, *Huit Catéchèses Baptismales* (ed. Wenger). English translation: Harkins, *Baptismal Instructions*.

before Communion because Communion was the central mystery of faith, and only those who had been initiated could witness the mysteries and take part. Sacred things required protection, so sacred things required responsible handling that required a level of knowledge and holiness. For that reason people spent three years as catechumens—learning the doctrines and ways of Christianity—before they were baptized.

Chrysostom's baptismal homilies were part of that process, and since their purpose was to provide people with their culminating address, the final words of encouragement and reality about what they were about to enter, the homilies are descriptions of the life they are committing to once they are baptized. That is, Chrysostom tells them what the Christian life is going to be like for them.

The two metaphors Chrysostom uses to describe the Christian life are marriage and military enlistment.[4] The first image is biblical—the church is the bride of Christ[5]—and Chrysostom fleshes out the metaphor to say that when a person is baptized he or she becomes Christ's bride. This person has a new identity and makes a total commitment to a whole new way of life, just as when a person marries. The second image conveys a similar idea: When a person is baptized, he or she joins up to Christ's people just like when enlisting in the military. No longer her own identity, she puts on a uniform and makes a commitment to a new way of life. Chrysostom preaches, "Forget your previous way of life, which led you into this shame. Make yourself forget all of those things and cast away from your mind all those mental pictures."[6] Chrysostom uses both images to emphasize the commitment and new identity a Christian

---

4. *Catech. illum.* 1.1 (SC 50:108; Harkins, *Baptismal*, 23).
5. Eph 5:22–24; Rev 21:2.
6. *Catech. illum.* 1.9 (SC 50:113).

takes on in baptism. To be a Christian means a particular way of living, and one needs to be committed to it. Even more important, one needs to know ahead of time what one is signing up for.

The other image that comes through in Chrysostom's baptismal homilies is of the Christian life as a battle with the devil in the arena. The passage is worth quoting in full in order to hear Chrysostom's own voice preaching to us:

> The Lord of angels presides as judge. This is not only an honor for us, but also a security. For when the one who laid down his life for us judges the wrestling match, what kind of honor is this? How much security? In the Olympic games the judge stands impartial from the competitors, favoring neither the one nor the other, but waiting for the result. . . . In our struggle with the devil, Christ does not stand impartial but is wholly on our side. . . . He anointed us with the oil of joy; he bound the devil with unbreakable chains in order to bind him hand and foot for the struggle. And if I slip, he reaches out his hand, lifts me up when I fall, and sets me on my feet again.[7]

Chrysostom says that during the catechumenate (the three-year period of preparation for baptism), everyone is in the training gym. They learn the devil's tactics and prepare strategies for evading and resisting. When they make mistakes or miss something, it is forgiven and something to learn from; it is not lethal. Their training, however, has been for the purpose of the real fight. When they come up out of the waters, they enter the arena and square off with the devil. As far as Chrysostom is concerned, the devil is always on the attack, attempting to deceive and tempt a

7. *Catech. illum.* 3.8–9 (SC 50:155–56).

Virtue, or the Christian Life

Christian away from God. We saw in the previous chapter that Chrysostom's insistence on the ascetic life is so much about staying vigilant, and this is what the vigilance is for. If anyone lets his focus slip for even a moment, the devil could get a grip on him. The good news, says Chrysostom, is that Christ is the judge of this contest, and Christ is not impartial. Christ is on our side. In fact, Christ has rigged the contest. Christ has bound the devil in chains hand and foot and then, when we do fall, Christ picks us up and puts us back on our feet.[8]

This image is why Chrysostom spends so much of his preaching urging his congregants to be vigilant and to live virtuously. The whole of the Christian life is a constant and unending—until heaven—struggle with the devil. The devil wants humanity's destruction, and virtue is resisting that destruction so that humanity—all of humanity—can flourish. Virtue is both the way *of* and the way *to* human flourishing for Chrysostom. Virtue is the way of life God ordained and the way of life in a Christian city described in the previous chapter. These things being what they are, Chrysostom reminds his audience every time he is in the pulpit that they need to be virtuous, need to live in ways that resist the devil's temptations and unmask his deceptions. Given his understanding that Christ has rigged the contest and is on our side, Chrysostom also says over and over that virtue is easy. Everyone can live this way. Because virtue is simply a matter of choice.

VIRTUE IS A CHOICE

Chrysostom agrees with all of his contemporaries that God created human beings free and self-determining.[9]

---

8. *Catech. illum.* 3.8–11 (SC 50:155–58; Harkins, *Baptismal*, 58–60).
9. Most of these discussions happen either when the author is

No one can force a person to do anything; everything is a free choice.[10] Nor can the devil or demons or angels force a person to do anything, and God will not compel either. He preaches, "[The devil] does not conquer with force, nor with tyranny, nor by compelling, nor by being violent. If this were the case, he would have destroyed all people."[11] Chrysostom is equally clear that God does not compel: "Since God loves humanity, beloved, and is beneficent, he creates and does all things so that we might shine with virtue. . . . He might persuade us to this, but he does not constrain or compel anyone."[12] The ability to choose resides with the person alone. Chrysostom's word for this is *proairesis* (προαίρεσις), which means "choice," and Chrysostom uses it as a technical term. The *proairesis* is the soul's capacity for choice, an aspect of human nature, that God has put in every person, and this capacity is untouchable.[13]

---

explaining how and why there is evil in the world or when discussing creation (if they are preaching on Genesis, for instance). For a sample of further reading, see Gregory of Nyssa, *Catechetical Oration* (*Oratio catechetica*), sections 5–7 especially: GNO 3.4.15–28. English: Gregory of Nyssa, *Catechetical Discourse* (trans. Green), 71–82. Methodius, *On Free Will* (better translated as *On Self-Determination*): *Peri tou autexousiou*, PO 22:789, ANF 6:356–64.

10. I use "free choice" and "self-determination" rather than "free will" because "free will" becomes weighted down with connotations and baggage during the debates Augustine had with the Pelagians in the early fifth century. Chrysostom is prior to those debates, and the conversations in the eastern part of the empire have a slightly different character than Augustine's account of free will does.

11. *Diab.* 1.1 (SC 560:122).

12. *Hom. Jo.* 10.1 (PG 59:73).

13. A related word is *gnome* (γνώμη), which means "mindset." Chrysostom often uses them together, though he will also use each separately to refer to some ability inherent in a person that is free and that no one can compel.

It lies at the center of every human being and is the place from which virtue and vice come.[14]

For Chrysostom this has to do with moral responsibility and God's justice.[15] If a person is punished for something she did not do, that would be unjust. If a person is punished for something she did but did not choose to do, that would be unjust. It is the reason the US has a category in its justice system for "not guilty by reason of mental defect": a person is held responsible only for things that she is able to choose to do. Or, as in many households, when I was a child my parents often told me I was being punished for hurting my brother because "I knew better," when supposedly my younger brother did not know better. Some kind of knowledge and ability to make a free choice is necessary to be responsible for a wrongdoing and therefore to be justly punished. The same is true of virtue: for a person to be praised for an action, she has to have knowingly and freely chosen that action, not been forced to do it.

Chrysostom takes this a step further in his account of human nature. He begins with the claim that God is both good and just. No Christians of the time would have disputed that claim. Therefore, if God is good and just, then any punishment or reward people receive for their behavior must be just. And if the punishment or reward is just, then the behavior has to have been freely chosen. So, Chrysostom says, God "everywhere threw out coercion, and highlighted choosing for oneself and self-determination."[16] God created human beings with souls that have the ability to choose freely.

---

14. Chrysostom also says that spiritual beings—angels and demons—have this free ability to choose (*proairesis*) as well.

15. Though there are similar themes in other writers, Chrysostom talks of responsibility more than others in these conversations.

16. *Hom Jo.* 10.3 (PG 59:76).

One way that Chrysostom talks about this is to say that there is a difference between nature and choice. If God had created human beings as morally evil by nature, that is, unable to do anything but evil because it is the nature they had, then no one could be held responsible for that evil. If God had created human beings as morally good by nature, that is, unable to do anything but good because of their nature, then no one could praise humans for doing any good.[17] Human beings are morally neither all good nor all evil by nature, however. They are free to choose their actions. As evidence, Chrysostom notes that no person always does evil things and no person always does virtuous things, and moreover, people are able to change. He preaches this as encouraging news: "Have you ever been bad, and have you ever also been good? . . . Did you at one time plunder things that didn't belong to you; and after that, overcome by pity, did you give of yourself to someone in need? Then where did this change come from? Is it not clear that it is from the mindset (*gnome*), and the choice (*proairesis*)?"[18] Whereas the apostle Paul was a Pharisee who persecuted Christians, he converted, changed, and became an apostle to the gentiles, himself eventually martyred as a Christian. The very existence of change in a person's life and actions means that virtue and vice are not part of our nature—the things about a person that are fixed and cannot be changed—but are results of our choices.

---

17. Yes, upon creating human beings—and all of creation—God did say, "it is good." God did create humans good, as good beings, but this is not a moral category. It is a statement about their ontological goodness. In terms of human nature, that nature is free and able to choose to do either good or evil.

18. *Hom. Matt.* 59.3 (PG 58:577).

VIRTUE IS "EASY" EVEN WHEN LIFE IS NOT

For Chrysostom, because virtue is a choice, virtue is easy. It is "just" a choice. Whatever the situation, it breaks down to some kind of choice a person can make. One of Chrysostom's main projects in preaching virtue is to take away his congregants' excuses for their sins. When he was in exile at the end of his life, Chrysostom sent back a treatise with one of his letters to Olympias, explaining that no one can harm another person without harming himself.[19] The crux of his argument is, again, that all human beings are free and have an ability to choose that cannot be compelled in any way. The responsibility for sin is the person's alone because the ability to choose sin is the person's alone. The argument begins by noting that there are two categories of harm that can befall a person: true harm and apparent harm.[20] By "apparent harm," Chrysostom means all kinds of suffering a person endures: starvation, oppression, financial strain, even murder. By "true harm," Chrysostom means sin: things God disapproves of and that breach the relationship between God and humanity. Sin is true harm because it is the only thing that can tarnish a person's virtue. Whatever suffering a person endures might be awful, but it cannot damage a person's virtue because virtue is a matter of choice, and nothing can make that choice but the person him- or herself. Chrysostom's three prime examples are Job, Cain, and Abel. Job remained virtuous even though he endured the epitome of suffering because he chose to stay faithful to God and not curse God. Abel was virtuous even though he

19. *Laed.* John Chrysostom, *Lettre d'exil à Olympias et à tous les fidèles (Quod nemo laeditur)*. English is *No One Can Harm the One Who Does Not Harm Himself*, NPNF[1] 9:269–84.

20. Chrysostom borrows Stoic categories and concepts here, but in the overall course of his work his version is distinctly Christian. For more on this, see Miller, *Chrysostom's Devil*, 118–23.

was murdered, so he suffered only apparent harm, not true harm; whereas Cain suffered true harm because he sinned in murdering his brother.[21] The sin caused damage.

Therefore, Chrysostom tells his audience, it does not matter what people do to you, nor what harm befalls you, your sin is your own. There is no excuse, no recourse to blame someone else; the sin is yours. As is your virtue. It appears that many in his audience tried to blame the devil for their sin, and Chrysostom tells them that no, in fact, the devil cannot make them sin because they have free choice. Even if the devil is tempting them by doing a seductive dance around an eighth slice of cheesecake, they are making the choice themselves to engage in gluttony.

This is another aspect of Chrysostom's preaching on virtue. For Chrysostom, virtue is not only a choice, but specifically a choice to resist the devil. I noted that the image of the Christian life Chrysostom gives to those about to enter that life is one of fighting with the devil in the arena. In this Chrysostom is similar to the monks: a Christian is one who fights off the attempts of the devil to pull a person away from Christ. For Chrysostom, a person is always either following Christ or following the devil; there is no in-between. To follow the devil is to be walking away from Christ, and to be resisting the devil is to be following Christ. This is why Chrysostom preaches vigilance so frequently. Vigilance is the first step in resisting the devil, and Chrysostom defines virtue in part as resisting the devil.[22]

---

21. "True" and "apparent" harm may not be the best categories for modern ears, as we might like to say that suffering is real harm, but they get at a helpful distinction.

22. For Chrysostom, as for everyone of his time, the world was populated by spirits as well as material creatures. The devil and his demons were real spiritual beings, not metaphors.

One additional aspect is that Christ makes obedience and resistance possible. In one place Chrysostom says that Christ has "made over" the faculty of choice (*proairesis*) so that it is possible to choose the good.[23] That faculty of choice was created free, but with sin it became harder to choose the good. Christ, in becoming human, makes it over so that it is better able to choose well. Further, in the arena image, Christ has bound the devil and is on the Christian's side. Should the Christian fall, Christ picks her up. For Chrysostom, Christ defeated the devil when he died and resurrected, and this changed the fight each Christian has with him. It means that every Christian can be victorious over the devil because Christ has already defeated him. In this way Chrysostom is a Christian rather than a Stoic.

HOW DOES ONE KNOW ONE IS VIRTUOUS?

One question this all raises is what constitutes virtue in a person? If virtue is about resistance and choice, does a person have to make a particular number of virtuous choices to be considered virtuous? Or is virtue dynamic rather than static? That is, can a person ever have the virtue or be the virtuous person Chrysostom urges them to be? Or is he encouraging them to be something he does not even believe is possible for them?

Chrysostom is not explicit or even all that clear on this question. When discussing what virtue is, he says it is "right actions of the soul" and "precision in true doctrine, and the

---

23. *Catech. illum.* 4.14 (SC 50:190): "The grace of God, having entered the souls, remolded and re-formed them and made them different from what they were, not changing their nature (*ousia*, οὐσία) but making over their choice (*proairesis*), . . . [and thereby grace] made them see precisely the ugly deformity of evil and virtue's shining beauty."

right way of life."[24] That is as explicit as he gets. In one place Chrysostom preaches, "Evil is nothing other than the disobedience of God,"[25] which suggests that Chrysostom also understands virtue in a Christian to be obedience to God, the "right way of life," the way of life God intends for human beings to live. And, as we have seen, living that right way of life, or having the right actions of soul, is a matter of choice, freedom, and responsibility. A person "just" needs to continue to choose obedience to God in every moment. The "precision in true doctrine" indicates that right belief is also part of virtue for Chrysostom, and he does preach occasionally on doctrinal matters to keep his congregation within orthodoxy. Notably, in the baptismal homilies, while explaining the new way of life and battle with the devil that Christians enter upon baptism, he does have a couple sections on the nature of the Trinity and what they believe as Christians. Still, the overwhelming majority of his corpus is focused on the way of living rather than ways of thinking or believing.

Sometimes Chrysostom calls his congregation to specific virtuous acts: reading the Bible, being chaste, and his favorite, giving alms and caring for the poor. Sometimes he is specific about sins people need to stop doing: frequenting the theaters and horse races, especially in place of attending worship. Most often, though, Chrysostom leaves the exhortation vague and lets his hearers apply the idea to the specific circumstances of their lives: "Let your virtue and your precise way of life and the righteousness of your deeds rouse those who see you to praise the common Lord of us all."[26]

From the various exhortations he makes for his audience to be virtuous, then, it appears that virtue is something a person can have and also can be, and virtue is dynamic

---

24. *Laed.* 5 and 3, respectively (SC 103:82, 70).
25. *Hom. Matt.* 59.3 (PG 58:577).
26. *Catech. illum.* 4.21 (SC 50:193).

rather than static. There are virtuous acts a person can do—reading the Bible, giving alms—and those things are the way God asks humanity to live, so they are being virtuous in doing those things. Similarly, resisting the devil is a substantial part of virtue, so every time a person resists the devil's temptation, she is virtuous. It seems that actively trying to be virtuous and being vigilant against temptation, deception, and sin make a person virtuous. There is not a particular level of these things above which a person is virtuous and below which a person is not. Continuing to make choices to live in obedience to God is living virtuously.

It is the continuous nature of this, however, that means virtue is dynamic. Because Chrysostom calls for constant vigilance and speaks of the battle with the devil always occurring—the devil is unwilling to give up—and tells his congregants they need to continue to make choices to do virtue, there is not a point at which a person is fully virtuous and can therefore stop. We do not reach a level and then hang out in virtue. It requires effort at all times, much like the gym, the image he uses in those baptismal homilies. A person must have habits and practices of virtue—like going to the gym—so that she is always ready to exercise her virtue. She has virtue as she builds her virtue. Because it requires constant effort and is not a static state, a person can also lose virtue. Chrysostom preaches, "[Pride] is enough for all the virtue of the soul to be destroyed completely, even if it finds almsgiving, prayer, fasting, whatever."[27] If virtuous actions are done for the wrong reasons—vainglory or pride, for instance—then the virtue is lost. In one place he says that chastity or choosing not to steal do not of themselves make a person virtuous; it is the whole way of life that does that. Yet Chrysostom in one place also refers to having

27. *Hom. Jo.* 16.4 (PG 59:106).

"pieces of virtue."[28] A person can have some virtue but not be complete in virtue. Even having pieces of virtue means a person is following Christ rather than the devil, and therefore is virtuous, though not perfectly so. Chrysostom does seem to believe that people can reach complete virtue, but he does not think there are all that many people who do.

CONCLUSION

Chrysostom preaches virtue as a struggle against the devil for obedience to God's way of life. This suggests that, for Chrysostom, Christians are always on the way to virtue and have pieces of virtue, attempting to gain more, reaching for complete and perfect virtue, rather than resting in some kind of static virtuous state. However, the constant struggle for virtue is also what makes a person virtuous.[29] That struggle is also entirely within the Christian's control because God has created every person with a capacity for free choice. No one can compel either sin or virtue, and, in fact, if a person were compelled and the choice were not free, then God would be unjust for either punishment or praise. Because of the soul's capacity for free choice, human beings are morally responsible. Therefore, Chrysostom preaches, "I urge you . . . be zealous for virtue. The pleasure of evil is brief, but the pain [of punishment] is incessant, but the joy of virtue is timeless, and the work is temporary."[30] We will see in a later chapter that virtue is important because it is what Christians bring to their salvation.

---

28. *Stat.* 20.8 (PG 49:210).

29. Louis Meyer describes Chrysostom's understanding of spiritual growth as that of a plant from a seed or the building of a house on a foundation, where the seed or the foundation is baptism (Meyer, *Saint Jean Chrysostome, maître de perfection chrétienne*).

30. *Hom. Jo.* 36.2 (PG 59:206); and *Laed.* 7 (SC 103:94–96).

DISCUSSION QUESTIONS

1. Why is being virtuous an all-or-nothing proposition for Chrysostom?
2. Why does Chrysostom focus almost exclusively on how to live the Christian life rather than preaching on Christian thought?

6

ALMSGIVING, WEALTH, AND POVERTY

THE THEME FOR WHICH John Chrysostom is probably best known is his unyielding insistence that everyone should give their money away. One scholar even calls him the "prophet of charity" because of the frequency with which Chrysostom ends his sermons by telling the congregation they need to give alms.[1] I call him an "anti-prosperity preacher."[2] It can sound as if Chrysostom is suggesting that it is not possible to be a good Christian with money, and definitely not with wealth. On occasion Chrysostom goes so far as to say that even being poor is not an excuse

---

1. Florovsky, "St John Chrysostom." In just his ninety Homilies on Matthew, Chrysostom referred forty times to almsgiving, thirteen times to poverty, thirty times to avarice, and twenty times to the abuse of wealth. See Brown, *Body and Society*, 309.

2. See Miller, *John Chrysostom and African Charismatic Theology*, 84.

for not giving alms. *Everyone* needs to give whatever they have. It is a matter of their virtue and their salvation.

GIVE!

As I wrote in chapter 2, the world Chrysostom inhabited was one where 10 percent of people were extremely wealthy, 10 percent were destitute poor, and the 80 percent in the middle were always one step from becoming destitute.[3] There was no middle class as we might think of it in the twenty-first-century United States.

One thing this means is that when Chrysostom preached about giving alms, he preached to people who lived in a world of poverty: both to the ruling rich in his imperial church who saw the poor at the church doors and, in greater proportion, to people we would think of as poor. People's resources were obvious, and there were no governmental structures or programs to help. Chrysostom preaches to people about almsgiving because people needed alms. The reality of the situation was clear to everyone. The poor were much less hidden than many of the poor in our own world. Poverty was on display in the city. In his sermons Chrysostom often chastises his congregants for stepping over the poor at the church door as they came in. He gets descriptive in one sermon on almsgiving, describing the beggars he walked past on his way to church:

> Coming through the marketplace ... hurrying to your assembly, I saw in the middle of the streets many outcasts, some with hands cut off, some with eyes gouged out, some filled with festering ulcers and incurable wounds. . . . I considered it

---

3. Brown, *Poverty and Leadership in the Later Roman Empire*, 14.

to be the worst inhumanity not to appeal to your love to talk about them.[4]

The beggars were right outside the church where the wealthy people who worshiped at Hagia Sophia in Constantinople, the emperor's church, came to listen to the golden-mouthed preacher. In one place Chrysostom tells his people that giving to those beggars should be part of the ritual of entering the church, just as washing one's hands before entering the church was part of the practice of making oneself ready for worship.[5]

CAN A WEALTHY PERSON BE A CHRISTIAN?

Let's deal first with a question that Chrysostom's strong words about wealth and almsgiving raises almost immediately: Can a Christian be wealthy? Is wealth an evil thing that leads people away from God? Or can a person use wealth rightly? My students and most US Christians I meet want very much for Chrysostom to allow them to have wealth. They want it to be about how they use what they have. That theme is there in Chrysostom, but he also has a lot of strong words about the temptation that wealth is.

Does Chrysostom think a Christian can be rich, or even "comfortable," as most people I know want to claim? Yes and no. Chrysostom preaches his sermons on Lazarus and the Rich Man, and there he is clear that it is our *choices* that make us virtuous, not our wealth, poverty, or other external circumstances (see previous chapter). He says that Lazarus is not virtuous because he is poor and the rich man is not vicious because he is rich. The rich man did not share his wealth, and that choice *did* make him vicious.

4. *Eleem.* 10.1 (PG 51:261).
5. *Paenit.* 3.2 (PG 49:294; Christo, *On Repentance and Almsgiving*, 33).

So in theory a Christian can have money and be virtuous because the money is external to the soul. Chrysostom even concedes that Job was a virtuous man with great wealth; it is not the wealth that makes a person virtuous, and poverty does not make a person vicious. Chrysostom calls his audience to pay attention to Lazarus's reward: "The rich [should pay attention], so you may not think that wealth without virtue is anything great; the poor [should pay attention], so you may not think that poverty is any evil."[6] Neither wealth nor poverty is a moral category.

More strongly, Chrysostom preaches:

> [Stop asking] why one such person is rich and another such person poor. For, asking these questions, you do the same thing as if going around to ask why one such person is white and another black, or one hook-nosed and another flat-nosed. For just as none of these things make a difference to us, whether it is this way or that way; in this way it is also nothing to be poor or to be rich, and much less than those other things. But the whole is about the way they are used. If you are poor, you can cheerfully live philosophically. If you are rich, you can be more miserable than all if you flee from virtue. For these make a difference to us, the things of virtue.[7]

This passage especially sounds like the views of faith and wealth held by wealthy Americans. However, it is not so simple to say that Chrysostom agrees with us. I do not think he does. Riches are temptations, according to Chrysostom, and they hinder salvation because they are temptations and distractions from God. And Chrysostom does not believe most Christians are capable of resisting the temptation and

6. *Laz.* 2.1 (PG 48:981).
7. *Hom. 1 Cor.* 29.6 (PG 61:248).

staying focused on God while holding wealth. Therefore Christians should give their money and goods away, so they do not have that temptation anymore.

Chrysostom preaches, "Let us not say that if God loved so-and-so, he would not have allowed him to become poor. This very thing is the greatest proof of God's love."[8] Poverty may not be virtue in itself, but poverty is a condition that allows for one to be closer to God because one is not distracted by the transitory things of this world. God loves that person so much that God has given him a head start on *apatheia* and attachment to God, if he so chooses. Yet Chrysostom also believes that the poor can be just as greedy as the rich. Poverty allows for attention to God, but it does not make it happen automatically. The person has to choose to respond that way.

Chrysostom also seems to think that most people who have wealth have gotten that wealth by unjust means. To those with generational wealth, he preaches: "Going back through all the generations, are you able to show that the acquisition is just? But it cannot be. The beginning of it and the root must be from some injustice. Why? Because in the beginning God did not make one person rich and another poor."[9] Even if the person gained wealth justly, Chrysostom says that to continue to be rich is a problem. He preaches, "Not to share with the poor out of our own wealth is theft from the poor and deprivation of their life; we do not possess our own wealth but theirs."[10] If a person has wealth, he is not using that wealth properly because he should be giving it to the poor. To have wealth is to keep others poor. If there are no more poor in the city, then a

---

8. *Laz.* 1.12 (PG 48:980).
9. *Hom. 1 Tim.* 12.4 (PG 62:563).
10. *Laz.* 2.6 (PG 48:992).

person can have wealth, but as long as there are beggars, no one should have wealth.

And yet, to complicate this further, Chrysostom praises Olympias for her faith. She is a wealthy widow who gives to the church and who is his dear friend. A wealthy person can be a Christian. He is also friends with other wealthy widows who give to the church but are wealthy enough that even in their giving they remain wealthy. According to Chrysostom, wealthy widows are Christians even though they are wealthy, often because of their giving and their chastity. Again, it appears that internal disposition is the key. If a person really can be not attached to her wealth, Chrysostom recognizes her faithfulness and virtue, but these widows are the only people Chrysostom speaks of in this category.

GIVING TO THE ECONOMIC VS. VOLUNTARY POOR

All these exhortations of Chrysostom's to give alms focus on the economic, or involuntary, poor rather than the voluntary poor. Those who had already given up everything to become ascetics also needed to rely on alms and others' resources to purse the ascetic life, but they had chosen this life. They had money and gave it away to live an ascetic life in pursuit of God. The economic poor were those whose circumstances were such that they did not have resources nor a way to gain resources for themselves. There was no choice about it. They worked hard, or they looked for work, or they were unable to work—perhaps from some physical or mental disability—and they could not survive without alms. These are the beggars outside the church.

That Chrysostom's constant exhortations to give are aimed at giving to the economic poor suggests that his congregants did not give in this way or that it was more important than giving to the voluntary poor. He even tells the poor themselves to give alms, and even these injunctions are about giving to the economic poor. People tended to see giving to the voluntary poor as helping with their own salvation, so people were already giving to the ascetics. The idea was that giving money or food to a monk would be met with prayers or some kind of heavenly merit to ensure salvation because the recipient of the alms was so holy.[11]

In contrast, Chrysostom says that giving to the economic poor aids the giver's salvation. Chrysostom discourages people from giving to ascetics precisely because they are ascetics. They are supposed to be poor: "If there is any ruler of the church who is living in abundance and does not want for anything, do not give to him, even if he is a saint, but prefer to give to the one who has need, even if he is not admirable. . . . If he is a saint but not in need, do not give."[12] Chrysostom includes bishops as voluntary poor because they are serving the church and meant to be also among the voluntary poor. They live in abundance because they have what they need. Chrysostom's people were to give to those who did not have what they need, in accordance with Christ's command to feed the hungry in Matthew 25's parable of the sheep and the goats.

An additional layer is that there was a moral connotation to poverty among Chrysostom's congregants. The poor were assumed to be frauds or lazy, even sinful.[13] Chrysostom insists that Christians give to them anyway, and even more, insists that a person's economic status does not reflect their virtue or lack thereof. In his homilies on the parable of Lazarus and the rich man, his most concentrated preaching on wealth and poverty, Chrysostom preaches, "Most people are in the habit, when they see someone in hunger, chronic

11. Brown, *Treasure in Heaven*, 36.
12. *Hom. Phil.* 1.5 (PG 62:188).
13. Mayer, "Poverty and Generosity," 150–51.

illness, and being in the extremes of sufferings, not to even allow him a good reputation, but they judge his life by his misfortunes and believe that he endures such suffering because of wickedness."[14] Chrysostom answers, "Let us not say that if God loved so-and-so, he would not have allowed him to become poor. This very thing is the greatest proof of God's love."[15] This coheres with Chrysostom's insistence that morality is about choice rather than external circumstances.

WHY GIVE

The people to whom Chrysostom insists his parishioners give indicates something about the reasons Chrysostom believes almsgiving is so important. Most simply, Chrysostom says Christians are to give because Christ said to feed the hungry and clothe the naked in Matthew 25. People have needs, and Christians are intended to meet those needs.

Beyond that simple reason, however, Chrysostom also explains the benefits of almsgiving to the giver. He goes to the heart of the issue in his commentary on Job:

> Possessions, the text says, are not of great importance for human beings. Let us listen, beloved .... [I]t is necessary to give away everything for the sake of our soul, and this is according to human nature, so that we will be robbed of any excuse when we blaspheme because of possessions. Possessions are nothing great, it says; for we give everything for the salvation of our own soul.[16]

Chrysostom spells it out: material possessions do not matter as much as the soul, so no one should be so attached to his

14. *Laz.* 1.10 (PG 48:977).
15. *Laz.* 1.12 (PG 48:980).
16. *Comm. Job* 2.4 (SC 346:162–64).

possessions that he would endanger his soul by not parting with something that another person needs, which Chrysostom names here as blaspheming because of possessions.

Chrysostom's strong appreciation for the parable of the sheep and the goats in Matt 25:31–46 is, I think, once more, behind this. Chrysostom reads that parable as though Christ means exactly what he says: any time a person gives alms, feeds the hungry, or clothes the naked, she does that for Christ himself, and eternal heaven is the reward, as promised in the parable. But to pass by the beggar in his need is to pass by Christ, and, as the parable has it, that person will suffer in hell for eternal punishment, the same hell designed for the devil.

To Chrysostom this should not be a difficult decision. He preaches, "Heaven is a trade and a business, and we are negligent. Give bread and take paradise. Give little things and seize great things. Give mortal things, and grab immortal things. Give corruptible things and capture incorruptible things."[17] The nature of all this wealth is transitory. In Chrysostom's mind, it is nonsensical to hold on to this ephemeral good when eternal good is within reach. There is no contest: give what cannot last if giving it will acquire what will last forever.

This is one of the more intriguing aspects of Chrysostom's rhetoric about alms. He often says things that sound as though almsgiving is salvific. Sometimes it can sound as though Chrysostom believes everyone needs to give alms in order to be a decent Christian. He comes off as rigid and intense. It can even sound as though giving alms is, for Chrysostom, one of the central acts that makes a person a Christian, somewhere not too far behind baptism.

---

17. *Paenit.* 3.2 (PG 49:294).

Almsgiving, Wealth, and Poverty

He preaches, "Almsgiving is the queen of the virtues, who quickly raises human beings into the vaults of heaven."[18]

Even more strongly, Chrysostom preaches, "If you have almsgiving as your advocate, even if you have many sins, do not be afraid. For not one higher power opposes her. She pays the debt [sin incurs]. She has her own bill that she holds in her hands.... Therefore, however many other sins you have, your almsgiving counterbalances the whole of them."[19] Something about this virtue in particular is more significant for Chrysostom than any other virtue. He speaks of virtue in general as a Christian's essential contribution to salvation (remember chapter 5, and see ahead to chapter 7), but he does not give any other virtue the pride of place he gives to almsgiving.

One thing to recognize is that early Christians were extremely attentive to post-baptismal sin. Chrysostom and his contemporaries spoke often about the danger of sinning after baptism. Christ has saved, and Christ has washed clean in baptism, but it is the Christian's duty to remain worthy of that salvation. They were all worried about what might wipe out sins committed after baptism.[20] It is possible that Chrysostom is talking about that here. Almsgiving would counterbalance all post-baptismal sins. Almsgiving pays the debt incurred in sin—not the initial cosmic debt incurred for all of humanity when Adam and Eve ate the fruit, for that was forgiven in baptism, but the debt racking up with further sins. There are places Chrysostom speaks of Christ's ongoing help in the struggle for post-baptismal virtue, so he does not think humans do this on their own, but he also

---

18. *Paenit.* 3.1 (PG 49:293).

19. *Paenit.* 3.1 (PG 49:293).

20. For an introduction to this topic, see Heine, *Classical Christian Doctrine*, 144–54.

thinks, along with his contemporaries, that almsgiving is a powerful enough virtue to pay that bill.

The language of almsgiving as leading to heavenly rewards is not unique to Chrysostom. Most of his contemporaries, including Augustine, talk about giving alms to the poor on earth in order to receive a heavenly reward.[21] For Chrysostom, as already mentioned, it is the parable of the sheep and the goats that is behind many of his discussions. Whatever a person gives to the "least of these" she gives to Christ, who then receives the giver into his heavenly kingdom. In one homily on almsgiving, Chrysostom says that the beggars a person gives to are Christ, and therefore such beggars, as Christ, are those who will stand in the final judgment and give an account of the Christian's actions or inactions.[22]

A QUESTION OF MOTIVATION

Given this strong language, someone may ask whether almsgiving can be a virtue if one gives in order to hasten her salvation. Would that not be selfish almsgiving? Possibly. We saw Chrysostom tell his congregants that almsgiving counterbalances all of their sins. Some of them may give to receive. Given that Chrysostom's training is in rhetoric (which we saw in chapter 3 is partly about persuading his hearers to live in particular ways) and that rhetoric is supposed to be able to bring about transformation, Chrysostom is probably trying to use rhetoric to convince his people to give. That is, he is knowingly speaking about the rewards for the purpose of motivation.

---

21. Helen Rhee offers a helpful introduction to this transactional rhetoric in early Christian discussions of alms in her Rhee, *Loving the Poor, Saving the Rich*, 73–102.

22. *Paenit.* 3.3 (PG 49:295–96; Christo, *On Repentance and Almsgiving*, 33–34).

Almsgiving, Wealth, and Poverty

The question, then, is whether selfish motivation negates the action of almsgiving.[23] For early Christians, Chrysostom included, motivation is secondary to action. It is important, but the first step is to do the action. Or at least, one's motivation is not an excuse not to give. Chrysostom does this with all sorts of virtues, not just almsgiving. His rhetoric is aimed at motivating behavior. So the act of giving is the essential thing because in giving, the giver practices letting go of attachments, practices prioritizing heavenly realities over earthly ones.[24] Chrysostom tells them to be concerned with their own souls, with their salvation, and almsgiving helps them with that. He does not say they have to do it for the right reasons in order to receive the benefits.

This further makes sense because of Chrysostom's emphasis on being able to control one's own virtue. That is the part the giver ought to be concerned with, and so that is the part Chrysostom focuses on. Chrysostom even tells his congregants not to worry about what the beggar will do with the money. To worry about whether the beggar

23. I offer that this question is not limited to almsgiving. If Chrysostom says that virtue is the contribution Christians bring to their salvation, then one could worry that working at any virtue is an attempt to hasten salvation. It is possible to do any virtue for selfish means, though the idea of almsgiving as paying for salvation is particularly abhorrent to people and so it stands out differently. I also offer that in Chrysostom's thinking, doing virtue is a response to salvation and an attempt to continue the work of one's salvation, not a matter of transactionally receiving salvation for a good deed.

24. Chrysostom speaks of heavenly realities and earthly realities, but he believes that Christians can live heavenly realities while on earth. He does not mean Christians should ignore their lives or the people around them. (If he did, he would not focus so much on helping the poor.) He means that Christians should be attached to God most firmly, while engaging their earthly realities and duties without being enslaved to them. This is why he says it is easier for monks to live the heavenly life: they can be more attached to God because they do not have the earthly realities the city folk do.

deserves it or will use it properly is to step into God's role, and that would be inappropriate.[25] The giver is to give because it contributes to her virtue and therefore her salvation, because Christ tells Christians to feed, water, clothe, and visit the least of these. It is the only part the giver can control, and so Chrysostom focuses on that.

Almsgiving is also essential for the receiver, and this may be part of why Chrysostom harps on it so much. Chrysostom would not tell people to give alms if there were no one to give *to*. There are people with need, and Christians are expected to meet needs. Regardless of motivation, the beggars need to eat, so Chrysostom insists that people give.

ALMSGIVING AS ASCETIC PRACTICE

Perhaps the strongest reason Chrysostom highlights the salvific nature of alms is that almsgiving is a letting go. It is, more than many virtues, a practice of detachment. We saw in chapter 4 Chrysostom's lifelong emphasis on asceticism, and asceticism is about loosening one's grip on earthly attachments in order to be attached only to God. Material realities are distractions from attention to God, and monks choose a life of poverty, which lightens them of worldly attachments and distractions. Almsgiving is one way that lay Christians in the cities can practice detaching themselves from wealth. They may not be choosing a life of poverty—to repeat, unless they were the 10 percent wealthy they were one step from poverty themselves—but they could practice giving rather than holding onto their resources. Chrysostom says this practice will lighten them, loosen their attachment to earthly things that distract from God.

---

25. See *Laz.* 2.5–6 (PG 48:989–90; Roth, *On Wealth and Poverty*, 52–55); *Eleem.* 6 (PG 51:269–70; Christo, *On Repentance and Almsgiving*, 146–49).

Even the poor are expected to give to those less poor. Poverty is no excuse, which tells us that it is not purely about the money. Regarding Paul's command to set aside something to give on the first day of the week (1 Cor 16:2), Chrysostom says this is not only for the rich but for everyone.

> By no means let poverty become an impediment to this contribution. Even if you are ten thousand times poor, you are not poorer than that widow who emptied herself of all she had. Even if you are ten thousand times a beggar, you are not more a beggar than the woman of Sidon who only had a handful of flour and was not kept from welcoming the prophet Elijah.[26]

This suggests that something more than wealth and poverty is at stake in almsgiving. It is ultimately about the way of the world God wants for his people.

In fact, as we saw in chapter 4, when Chrysostom tells his congregants to imitate the monks and live ascetic lives in the city, he concedes that it is harder for people in the city to live a virtuous life focused on God than it is for the monks precisely *because* city folk have more distractions. One who has given up all his possessions has fewer temptations. Therefore, almsgiving would also remove temptations. In his *Comparison Between a King and a Monk*, Chrysostom highlights the superiority of the monk over kings and wealthy men. The root of the superiority is the monks' voluntary poverty because it means there are fewer distractions from the heavenly life God intends. Chrysostom writes, "Wealth is transitory, and what seems to be good perishes along with this life," but what the monk has, his way of life, "these things are truly good and saving and lasting, through the philanthropy and providence of

---

26. *Eleem.* 3 (PG 51:265).

Christ."[27] The goal of all is to imitate the monks, who show the form of life all Christians ought have, one of detachment from the world through a voluntary poverty.

Chrysostom may also highlight almsgiving because of its communal nature. Chrysostom's goal is the transformation of the whole city, so giving to those who do not have enough transforms the city into a place where everyone has enough. In a homily on Matthew where he again tells his audience to imitate the monks, Chrysostom describes the monastic life as communal, writing, "There is one table for everyone, both for those who are served and for those who serve; the same food, the same clothes, the same home, the same way of living. . . . There is not 'mine' and 'yours,' but this expression that is the cause of myriad wars is banished."[28] In his early treatise *Against the Opponents of the Monastic Life*, Chrysostom says that the commonality of monastic life imitates the life of the angels in heaven: "Just as among the angels there is no inequality, nor do some enjoy prosperity while others experience misery, but all of them share one peace, one joy, one glory, so it is likewise in the monasteries."[29] What this means is that Chrysostom envisions the heavenly life as one where there is no inequality. That is the life Christians are aiming for, and almsgiving brings them closer to this life as those with resources provide for those without so that all have the same peace, joy, and glory. As I will talk about in chapter 7, Chrysostom's vision of salvation is not individual but communal. Almsgiving as a virtue is part of that vision too.

So when a person is able to be detached from wealth, or even just from the general everyday things of this world, Chrysostom says she will more readily be able to care for

27. *Comp. reg. mon.* 4 (PG 47:392; Hunter, *Comparison*, 76).
28. *Hom. Matt.* 72.3 (PG 58:673).
29. *Oppugn.* 3.11 (PG 47:366; Hunter, *Against*, 147).

the poor. The detachment does not lead to less care or less involvement in the world but more. Chrysostom preaches:

> One who can philosophize about the resurrection and move himself entirely to the future life will consider present things nothing: neither wealth, nor abundance, nor gold, nor silver, nor the covering of clothes, nor delicacies, nor expensive tables, nor any other such thing. And the one who considers these things to be nothing will more willingly stand as a guardian of the poor.[30]

The point of asceticism is to live in the order of flourishing for everyone that God created. Giving alms brings both the giver and receiver more into that flourishing.

CONCLUSION

Chrysostom preached at length and in many sermons about giving alms to the poor. He says that everyone needs to give. He says that giving is a means to salvation. He is clear that giving is to be for the involuntary, rather than the voluntary, poor, which tells us that giving is about making sure that everyone has what they need. Yet Chrysostom has to motivate his people to give, so he speaks about the salvific rewards of almsgiving for the giver.

For Chrysostom, wealth and poverty are about what is temporary versus what is eternal. Almsgiving is a practice that helps a Christian rely less on temporary things and attend more to eternal realities. Wealth and poverty are not in themselves indicators of virtue or vice, but the choices a person makes about their wealth or poverty do constitute virtue and vice, just as we saw in the previous chapter. All virtue comes down to choice, rather than external circumstances.

---

30. *Eleem.* 1 (PG 51:262).

When all people make virtuous choices, the city itself becomes a heavenly city, a communal vision of salvation.

DISCUSSION QUESTIONS

1. What are the passages of Scripture most germane to Chrysostom's thought on almsgiving (i.e., Matthew 5, 25; Luke 6, 16)? What challenges do they offer us?

2. What do you think of Chrysostom's seeming unconcern with what might be seen as the transactional nature of almsgiving?

7

SALVATION

The reason Chrysostom spends so much time telling people to be virtuous, the reason he insists that they give alms as a means of being virtuous, the reason he encourages them all to live ascetic lives aiming at *apatheia* and the angelic life is because all of these things are finally, for Chrysostom, about salvation. He cares for his congregants' salvation and says that they should too. In fact, he often urges them, "Do not think too little of your salvation!"[1] Everything he preaches is somehow about his attempt to bring his congregants to their salvation and prevent their eternal destruction.

SALVATION IS A COOPERATIVE VENTURE

For John Chrysostom, salvation is a cooperative venture between the Christian and God. God has done all the heavy lifting, but the Christian still needs to sweat. Chrysostom

---

1. *Hom. Gen.* 8.6 (PG 53:75–76).

often tells his congregation that salvation is composed of two parts: God's part and their part. This statement from one of his homilies on Romans is representative: "Contemplate with me how everywhere Paul puts down these two things: both what is up to him [Christ], and what is up to us."[2] God has designed salvation so that there are things God is responsible for and also things humans are responsible for.

The reason for this cooperative design is for God to preserve human freedom and self-determination. Yes, God could unilaterally save humans, but that would neither respect nor preserve the freedom and autonomy God created them with in the first place. Chrysostom observes in one of his homilies on Hebrews that "all things depend on God, but not so that our self-determination is harmed.... It is up to us, and it is up to Him."[3] God stops short of taking away our freedom to choose and to act because it is the capacity he created us with in the beginning. Moreover, to encroach on human freedom would be to remove the possibility of God's justice or fairness, as we saw in chapter 5. Therefore, in order to preserve God's justice, Chrysostom says that just as no one, the devil included, can compel another person's choice, neither will God do so. Thus, God assigns part of humans' salvation to them and does not do it all for them.

The other way that Chrysostom speaks of the reason for this design is represented by this description in one of his Ephesians homilies:

> [Paul] says, "In love, having preordained us." For this [preordination] comes not from efforts, nor from good works of ours, but from love; and yet not of love alone, but also of our virtue. For if indeed from love alone, it would be necessary

2. *Hom. Rom.* 9.2 (PG 60:468).
3. *Hom. Heb.* 12.3 (PG 63:99).

Salvation

> for all to be saved; but again, if from our virtue alone, then his coming [the incarnation] was superfluous, and all his economic works. But it is from neither his love alone, nor from our virtue, but from both.[4]

Chrysostom explains to his audience the logical consequences if salvation were either all God's work or all humans' work. If it were God only, his love deciding to save, then everyone would have to be saved because God's love wills for all to be saved. But Chrysostom notes elsewhere that Scripture insists not everyone will be saved, at least as he interprets it.[5] He spends a lot of time telling his congregants about hell in great detail in order to scare them into caring enough about their salvation to participate in it with their virtue.[6] Therefore, Chrysostom argues that if salvation were only a matter of God's love, all would have to be saved, but since Scripture tells him that not everyone is saved, God's love is not the only part.

Chrysostom continues on to explain that neither is salvation only a matter of a person's virtue. If it were only about a person's virtue, then the incarnation would be "superfluous." There would have been no reason for God to become flesh, let alone all the other works God did, including Christ's death and resurrection. Since God did become flesh, Chrysostom says that salvation cannot be only up to humans. Otherwise why would God have done such a drastic thing? It would not make sense. Thus, says Chrysostom,

---

4. *Hom. Eph.* 1.2 (PG 62:12).

5. Chrysostom is especially fond of Matt 25:31–46, which he takes to mean that people who have followed the devil rather than Christ will find themselves in hell for eternity.

6. For more on Chrysostom's propensity to this, see Miller, "Hellish Homiletic Practices."

logic dictates that salvation is both from God's love and from human virtue.

Those, then, are the two parts: God's love and human virtue. The first part is God's part, or the things of salvation that are "up to God." In some places Chrysostom names these things as God's love and in other places as Christ's incarnation, death, and resurrection. This part of salvation is primary. Without God's action, no human action or virtue would matter. God's work in Christ is prior to any human contribution and makes the human's contribution possible at all.

Chrysostom's descriptions of Christ's work are common among the many descriptions of Christ's work by his contemporaries. Chrysostom may speak of Christ "fettering" the devil when the devil overreached his purview by trying to take the innocent Christ and so bringing punishment on himself.[7] Another common description uses language of reconciliation, of God reaching out to reconcile himself to humanity even though God was the one who was wronged. Chrysostom preaches, "God is the one who works the whole, who reconciled the world through the Only-Begotten. And how did he reconcile it to himself? . . . Forgiving their sins; for there was no other way. . . . But even though our sins were so big, not only did he not demand justice, he even reconciled."[8] "There was no other way" for reconciliation between God and humanity to happen but that God forgave humanity's sins. And so God did. God, through Christ, reconciled the world back to himself by forgiving their sins. Chrysostom goes into no further detail here about what these things mean or how it happened, just

---

7. For a good initial and accessible overview of ancient theories of the atonement, see chapter 11 in Heine, *Classical Christian Doctrine*, 116–28.

8. *Hom. 2 Cor.* 11.2 (PG 61:477).

that God forgave in Christ and that this action of God was necessary.

Elsewhere Chrysostom says a little bit more, though he is still vague about the mechanics of salvation. It seems that the thing he most wants his congregants to know is that Christ's death and resurrection effected the reconciliation of all people with God. That is, Christ's death and resurrection achieved salvation for humanity. In general, Chrysostom emphasizes Christ's death more than his resurrection. For Chrysostom Christ's resurrection is the model for human resurrection, but Christ's death is the reason Christians are reconciled and will enjoy a heavenly life. In a representative statement, and one that is standard among his contemporaries, Chrysostom preaches, "Christ himself being in death, he in this way overcame it so as to raise up those who were already held down by it."[9] By dying, Christ overcame death altogether so that all humans, made mortal when they ate the fruit God commanded them not to eat, could become immortal again.[10]

There is also a strand of thought about the atonement that says all human beings deserve death because of their sin—Chrysostom means the sin of Adam and Eve—but that Christ died in their place. He preaches, "See how he became

---

9. *Hom. Jo.* 5.3 (PG 59:58).

10. For a more detailed discussion of the possible atonement theories Chrysostom endorsed, see Barnard, "Christology and Soteriology in the Preaching of John Chrysostom," 153–210; and Lawrenz, "Christology of John Chrysostom," 177–200. Both authors conclude that *Christus victor* is the most accurate description of Chrysostom's beliefs but allow for elements of other theories, in particular, the ransom theory. The primary difficulty with both authors, though Barnard is the more egregious offender, is that they apply theories to Chrysostom's thought anachronistically rather than describing Chrysostom's understanding. Though they rigorously investigate his understanding, they spend too much time and effort attempting to overlay more recent theories onto Chrysostom.

a mediator . . . he [Christ] died on our behalf and made us worthy of the trust (*diathekes*)."[11] Christ is a mediator first, moving between God and humanity to bring us God's messages and to "carry" us to God, and since that is not sufficient for humanity's salvation, Christ also dies for humanity, in their place, to make them worthy of the covenant God made with them, since humanity was not able to make themselves worthy of it. I will come back to Chrysostom's frequent use of "worthy" language in a moment.

So much for God's part. When Chrysostom says that human beings have to bring something to their salvation, he talks about their contribution either as faith or as virtue. When he speaks of the Christian bringing faith to her salvation, he means proper doctrine, and usually the places where he says this explain that a Christian needs to believe the Trinitarian doctrine that God is Father, Son, and Holy Spirit and to believe in accordance with the Nicene Creed, which had been affirmed and expanded at the Council of Constantinople just a few years before Chrysostom was ordained. In most of the places Chrysostom does this he is addressing a particular errant Arian belief that had been rejected at the Councils of Nicaea and Constantinople.[12] The exception is in one of his early baptismal homilies, where he takes a few minutes to explain the nature of God as Trinity to those about to be baptized. For Chrysostom, correct thinking about God is one part of what Christians bring to their salvation.

---

11. *Hom. Gen.* 8.6 (PG 53:75). *Diathēkēs* (διαθήκης) is also the word used for "covenant" in the NT and the Septuagint (the Greek translation of the Hebrew Old Testament).

12. Arians believed that the Father created the Son and therefore the Son was not the same substance as the Father. Chrysostom in these passages is trying to affirm the orthodox position on the Trinity that the Father, Son, and Spirit are all of the *same substance* and are equal.

More often than telling his congregants to bring their faith, however, Chrysostom tells them they must contribute their virtue to Christ's work in order to receive salvation. Often he phrases this as proving worthy of their salvation. For instance, "Let us be in awe of the excess of grace offered to us by God . . . so that, having contended lawfully . . . we may be worthy of those great crowns."[13] I'll address below the question of whether this is some kind of works-righteousness, but here let me simply say that Chrysostom usually means that Christ has made human beings worthy of all the good God has for them. Christ does this (i) through his own sacrifice and resurrection and (ii) through baptism, as it unites Christians to his death and resurrection. And the Christian's job is to remain worthy. Sometimes Chrysostom says their job is to keep their baptismal robe gleaming white.

All those exhortations to be virtuous that we explored in chapter 5, all the insistence that each person has a faculty of choice (*proairesis*) that cannot be compelled, and therefore each person has responsibility for her choices and actions—all of that is aimed at this larger goal of salvation. That a person is responsible for her virtue means that she can be rewarded for her virtue. If virtue were somehow able to be forced, a person would not be responsible for it and therefore could not receive heavenly rewards because she would not be the one who was truly virtuous. This is the reason Chrysostom so emphasizes virtue among his congregants—it is a necessary element for their salvation. Thus Chrysostom often preaches versions of the statement "Let us not think too little of our salvation!"[14]

Yet even here, virtue requires help from God. Even when a person attempts to bring his virtue to bear on his

13. *Hom. Gen.* 8.6 (PG 53:75).
14. This one comes from *Hom. Gen.* 8.6 (PG 53:75–76).

salvation, he must be cooperating with God, or it will not matter. Chrysostom says, "A person's willingness (*prothymia*/προθυμία) is not sufficient, unless there is some beneficial tipping of the scale from above; and that again we gain nothing by the tipping of the scale from above, if there is not a willingness.... For from these two things virtue is woven."[15] Both divine and human action are necessary, not only for salvation but also for completing the virtue that is a necessary contribution to salvation.

CHRYSOSTOM IS NEITHER A PROTESTANT NOR A HERETIC

In all of this, twenty-first-century Protestants tend to hear that Chrysostom believes people have to earn their salvation. That is not at all the case. We hear this because Protestants have been trained to reject anything at all that sounds like salvation is about anything other than completely unearned grace because of the particular doctrines and behaviors Martin Luther was rejecting in the sixteenth-century Catholic Church. This misunderstanding becomes especially acute, as I noted above, when Chrysostom's language of worthiness comes in.

Chrysostom's articulation of salvation was completely normal in his time and among his contemporaries. Yes, Chrysostom tells his people that they have to contribute to their salvation with their faith and virtue, and that not adding those things to Christ's work will see them suffering the

---

15. *Hom. Matt.* 82.4 (PG 58:742). An example of a situation where Chrysostom sees this working is Joseph's resistance of the advances of Potiphar's wife. He writes, "This man, after doing what he could and demonstrating his struggle for chastity with great intensity, enjoyed much help from on high and had victory in the struggle by cooperation [*symmachias*/συμμαχίας] from God's right hand" (*Hom. Gen.* 62.4 [PG 54:538]).

greatest torments in hell, but this is not to say that anyone is "earning" their salvation. In fact, Luther would have agreed with this much, since he thought that people could end up in hell also, based on what they believed. Chrysostom insists that God's work is *prior to* the human's work and *more significant*. Without Christ's death and resurrection, there is no salvation for anyone. This is the necessary condition, and it must precede any human action.

Chrysostom uses the phrases "up to us" and "our part" and "what we bring or contribute" to salvation, suggesting that though God has done the major work, there is something for humanity to do as well, in addition or in response to that work. Further, Chrysostom says that God designed salvation this way so that human beings could show their effort and, more importantly, so God would respect human freedom and self-determination, with which he created them in the first place. In this way, God is just because any punishment or reward is just, since the human being made a choice for himself. For God to save unilaterally would not be just, in Chrysostom's understanding.

Since Christ's work is the primary and major component, Chrysostom is not suggesting that a person can earn her salvation, certainly not on her own. Christ has already offered salvation to everyone, regardless of how virtuous they are. In fact, in his baptismal homilies, Chrysostom is vivid in his description of how unworthy of salvation human beings are. He uses the metaphor of marriage to explain baptism, and he says that Christ marries the Christian even though the Christian is a hideously ugly bride, soiled in all kinds of ways.[16] It is Christ's choice of the hideous bride while in the condition of her unworthiness that implies neither ability nor need to make oneself worthy. Christ

---

16. For instance, this passage: *Catech. illum.* 1.3 (SC 50:110; Harkins, *Baptismal*, 24).

makes one worthy, and then the Christian must keep herself worthy by means of her virtue. So Chrysostom insists a person must participate in his salvation and has need to contribute to his salvation, but these are not the same as earning one's salvation.

CAN EVERYONE BE SAVED?

Given this structure, then, does Chrysostom believe that everyone can be saved, as long as they contribute their virtue? In short, yes. Chrysostom preaches to his congregants, "Do not think too little of your salvation! Nothing is as important as virtue."[17] That he preaches this to everyone suggests that he believes everyone can receive salvation. As I described above, everyone has to participate in their salvation, so even as the onus of action is on the Christian—because God has already done God's work in salvation, and it covers everyone—it is *possible* for everyone. God does the work of incarnation, death, resurrection, renewing-human-nature, and he does them for everyone. And everyone can add their part to this base.

The difficulty is whether everyone *does* add their part. As we saw, Chrysostom believes virtue and faith are the things Christians contribute to that base. Chrysostom preaches sometimes about correct doctrine and faith, so he knows that not everyone believes properly, and that means some people will not receive their salvation because of the faith—identified as correct belief rather than amount of faith—they do not hold.

Far more often, however, Chrysostom's exhortations "Do not neglect your salvation!" are about his congregants' virtue. We saw in chapter 5 that virtue is dynamic in people, but because it is "simply" a matter of choosing the virtuous

17. *Hom. Gen.* 8.6 (PG 53:75–76).

thing over and over, and because choice is free in every human and unable to be compelled, everyone is able to make that choice. Therefore, salvation is available to everyone because God has accomplished his saving acts for everyone and because everyone is able to choose to add their virtue to God's work.

Chrysostom does not, however, give a rubric for what constitutes "enough" virtue when he says that every Christian must contribute their virtue or else neglect his salvation. He insists all the time that they be vigilant so as not to be deceived or fall into temptation, to thereby lose the virtue they had. Often he tells them that it is laziness or inattentiveness that brings the fall away from virtue.[18] This insistence on vigilance suggests that it is the attempt to remain in virtue that matters. Every choice to virtue turns a person toward Christ (and away from the devil), and therefore makes her virtuous. We will not be able to pin him down to a precise definition on this question. We will have to be content with knowing that Chrysostom does believe that everyone *can* receive Christ's salvation but he does not believe that everyone *does*.

THE SAVED LIFE BEGINS NOW

One last important aspect of Chrysostom's soteriology is that Chrysostom believes a person's salvation begins now, in the present life, and is not merely waiting passively for heaven. Talking about baptism while discussing Romans 6, Chrysostom preaches:

> Having believed that Christ died and that he was raised, therefore you must also believe your own

---

18. See Leyerle, *Narrative Shape of Emotion*, 150–54, on Chrysostom thinking laziness (*hrathymia*/ῥαθυμία) is the original sin. Cf. Lai, "Vision of the Angelic Life."

> [death and resurrection].... For if you shared in death and burial, much more you will share in resurrection and life.... After the future resurrection has been set before us, [Paul] demands of us another resurrection, the new way of life [*politeian*/πολιτείαν], which is borne in our present life by a change of our habits.[19]

Christians are united to Christ in resurrection because of his own resurrection, and that resurrection is not only a future reality but a present one. Chrysostom says that those who have received Christ's salvation and become part of the church in baptism (become Christian) rise with Christ to a new life even now. He describes this as a "new way of life," a *politeia* (πολιτεία).

It is a big deal for Chrysostom that people can change. If they could not become better, then their morality would be part of their nature and something they would not and could not be responsible for. They can change, though. Paul is his greatest example of this transformation. The once-persecuting Paul became the epitome of Christian faithfulness and virtue, according to Chrysostom, which demonstrates both the power of Christ and the freedom of human beings to make their own choices about virtue.

In the passage here, Chrysostom says that Paul explains the future resurrection Christians can expect because they have been united to Christ's resurrection, Christ pulling them up with him, and then Chrysostom says that Paul also demands a present resurrection. Christians must change their habits and live in a new way of life. The *politeia* Chrysostom mentions is a theme in his writings. *Politeia* is the Greek word for city as well as for way of life (as in the ordered way of life in a city, which comes to mean the way a person lives day to day), and Chrysostom insists that there

---

19. *Hom. Rom.* 10.4 (PG 60:480).

is a Christian *politeia*, that is, a Christian way of living that is for individuals and also for a Christian city. His goal is that all Christians live in the virtue Christ enables and thus transform the city into a Christian city. That would be, according to Chrysostom, heaven on earth.

Living in the heavenly city on earth, or, as Chrysostom often phrases it, living the "heavenly way of life" on earth, is what salvation looks like for Chrysostom. And the people who are doing this best in his view are the monks. They are conversing with angels and with God in modes of friendship. They live well-ordered existences. In short, he says, the monks live the heavenly life now here on earth. Moreover, this heavenly life they live is the one that God intended for everyone to live from the beginning. It is the life Adam and Eve experienced before the fall.

All of the ancient Christians understood that salvation was about restoring humanity to the way of life God wanted them to have from the beginning. God intended their flourishing. Christians see that divine intention in Genesis in the story of the garden when God walks with Adam and Eve. That idyll is what the virtuous life—in participation with the work Christ did in death and resurrection—returns humanity to. Christians can once again live in intimate relationship with God. It is a matter of them choosing the virtuous way of life day after day, which is possible because Christ has done the work to renew human nature.[20]

The mark of this life, for Chrysostom, is *apatheia*, an imperturbability of spirit regardless of one's life circumstances. Therefore, as we saw in chapter 4, the monks are the example of the saved life. *Apatheia* is the goal of the ascetic life, and Chrysostom says it is what the angels have. More significantly Adam and Eve had this "*apatheia* of the angels"

20. For more on this, see Miller, *Chrysostom's Devil*, 136–38, 146–52. See also Douglas, "Easy Virtue."

before the fall, and it was the thing that distinguished their peaceful, abundant, free existence.[21] The monks struggle through their ascetic disciplines and practices in this life to attain *apatheia*, and since they must remain vigilant always lest they fall away from their virtue and thus their *apatheia*, there is always some struggle, but when they are living in *apatheia*, Chrysostom says they live in a kind of rest. The struggles and difficulties of this life do not shake those with *apatheia*; they float above the struggles. Still, because they are working to stay in this state, they look forward to the final heavenly rest, which will be a true rest.

The monks in this heavenly rest on earth are models of the present dimension of salvation. They are contributing their part—their faith and virtue—to God's prior work, and by doing so they receive salvation now. They do not have to wait for death and heaven. Their rest and reward will be increased in heaven, but they get to enjoy the fruits now. And, in the same way, all Christians can live the life intended for them, even now.

CONCLUSION

Chrysostom's view of salvation is that God does all the most important work, and humans need to contribute their faith and virtue to that work to receive salvation. God becomes human in Jesus; Jesus dies; and Jesus rises from the dead, all of which renew human nature and allow and enable the Christian to live in friendship with God. To this work the Christian needs to add her own faith—correct doctrine was essential for Chrysostom—and her virtue, which Chrysostom spends a lot of time encouraging in his congregation. The virtuous Christian will imitate the monks, who are already imitating the angels and living the saved life now

21. *Hom. Gen.* 17.1 (PG 53:134).

on this earth. Waiting passively for heaven is not how salvation works for Chrysostom. Were one to do that, she would neglect and therefore lose her salvation. Instead, one's salvation begins now, with the earthly heavenly life. Pursuit of virtue is the path, and a restored flourishing as was meant for everyone in the beginning is the reward.

DISCUSSION QUESTIONS

1. Chrysostom says that Christians participate in their salvation as a response to God's work in Christ. How do you think about participation in salvation? Do you need to offer anything? Why or why not?

2. What ought the world look like if salvation does begin now? How ought we be living? How is this both individual and communal?

3. Chrysostom speaks of the saved life as an angelic life. What does that mean to you? What would an angelic existence on earth look like? What would friendship with God be? How would you work toward that?

8

PROBLEMS

Two themes in Chrysostom's preaching and writing are problematic: his views of women and his anti-Semitism. Both permeate his writing, both are entirely consistent with the views of other Christian authorities of Chrysostom's time, and both are themes that chafe many modern readers. In an introduction to John Chrysostom's thought I would be remiss if I did not acknowledge these two themes, since any reader who is motivated by this book to go read some Chrysostom for herself is going to find these thoughts quickly. Yet it is not enough to acknowledge them in a sort of warning. In a book where I suggest that Chrysostom is worth learning from still today, I need to note the things I hope we will *not* listen to. But then it is necessary to tackle the question: What do we do with these thoughts and teachings of Chrysostom's? How do we learn from Chrysostom in a complex way that recognizes beliefs that are no longer acceptable to Christians? How do we discern what to keep and what to lose? And what do we do with the material we discern is "not of God"?

This is an important question. One of my family members often says something along the lines of, "I can't believe they took down the statue of that person! His beliefs were totally normal at the time. We can't judge him by the moral standards of our own time." In one sense this family member is right; the historical figure was a product of his time, and by the moral standards of his time and place—for moral standards are culturally located—his beliefs were considered acceptable. Yet if I cannot say that those beliefs were problematic, how can I say that sexism is wrong? For I do not merely want to claim that sexism is wrong today; I also want to claim that it was wrong even when people did not believe it was wrong. And yes, this is as understood by my own time and place. There are cultures in the world in my own time that would define sexism differently, and adjudicating between them is as difficult as adjudicating between times.

I do not suggest there is either an easy or a simple solution to this quandary, but it is worth wrestling with the question. How can I say that Chrysostom's sexism or anti-Semitism is not part of what we should learn from Chrysostom about living with God into greater holiness? The answer is going to require some theology and a recognition that God is growing the church into holiness, but we are not there yet.[1] We recognize that we are all doing our best, and some of our best will not be right. This means also that we have to hold our own theology and preaching loosely enough to be corrected, to think that we might not have it all right either.

---

1. On the question of tradition including sin as well as holiness, see Carpenter, *Nothing Gained Is Eternal*. If Christian history is all the actions of all the Christians of all the times and all the places, then there is sin as well as truth being transmitted by tradition because human beings are sinful. Carpenter suggests a way forward in discerning and working.

First, let me note what Chrysostom says about women and about Jews. Let me point out where he says things and how, so we can see more clearly what he believes. I will point out how Chrysostom's thinking is common to men of his position and time. Then I will suggest how we might deal with these elements of Chrysostom's thought in our own reading, especially as his beliefs did not die in his own era. These thoughts have persisted in many iterations of Christianity in various times and places, and there are Christians who believe similar things today. All of this is to say that engaging with Chrysostom will open into the greater question of how we engage with theology of any century in order to be transformed into a better image of Christ.

CHRYSOSTOM'S WORDS ABOUT WOMEN

It is too strong to call Chrysostom's views on women misogynist.[2] He had good relations with many women, both ascetics and non-ascetics; he wrote letters with women throughout his time in both Antioch and Constantinople; he trusted women with some administrative work; he was good friends with some women, notably Olympias. Scholarly consensus now is that Chrysostom was not a misogynist. However, his views of women and the nature of women do reflect his existence as a fourth-century male theologian in power. For that reason, it can be hard to read some of his words now.

One theme in Chrysostom's discussions of women is that they care more for jewelry than for their souls. He likes to contrast virtue with appearance and will speak of women

---

2. For an overview of the current state of scholarship on just how misogynistic Chrysostom actually was, see Mayer, "John Chrysostom and Women Revisited." For a lengthier overview of the subject of Chrysostom about women in general, see Walsh, "Overcoming Gender."

as obsessed with their accessories but not worrying about their virtue.³ As he prepares people for baptism, Chrysostom preaches:

> From now on let there not be attention to external enhancements and expensive clothes but let all zeal be toward the beauty of the soul, so that it may become a brighter beauty.... I wish you women to abstain ... from plastering your face and adding to them as if the craftsmanship were defective.... You add nothing to your face from this work, but you will destroy the beauty of your soul.⁴

After baptism, Chrysostom says, women need to care only for their souls' virtue, not for the virtue of their faces. Putting energy to one's face or one's clothing is energy spent on transitory realities, not eternal ones. Physical beauty does not matter, but the beauty of the soul does, and taking time away from concern for soul beauty is dangerous. Chrysostom explains this at the outset to those about to become Christians. He is explaining the Christian life, and he wants them to know that the Christian life is about virtue of soul.

In some places Chrysostom speaks of the desire for beauty as not only frivolous and a problem because it distracts from effort toward real virtue but also because makeup and accessories were for the purpose of adultery

---

3. Perhaps most famously, Chrysostom tells the empress publicly that she cares too much about her finery. I spoke in chapter 1 about how this is not the real reason for his exile, but it persists as legend. Supposedly in a homily on Colossians, where Chrysostom contrasts the golden chains women wear as jewelry with the chains of Paul, Chrysostom pointed at the empress and made people to understand that this was a statement about her. See *Hom. Col.* 10.4 (PG 62:371). For discussion of this legend, see Kelly, *Golden Mouth*, 150.

4. *Catech. illum.* 1.34, 37 (SC 50:125, 127).

and prostitution, and because it increases lust in men.⁵ Chrysostom thinks that beautification can be sinful, not only a neutral distraction. Bound up with this is the idea that women are frivolous and more easily tempted than men, which is part of Chrysostom's second major theme regarding women.

The other major dimension of Chrysostom's understanding of women is that women are by nature weaker than men. Physically, yes, and also mentally and emotionally. The belief that women are not as strong as men or as capable was a common understanding of Chrysostom's time (and is still a belief in some strands of Christianity). Gregory of Nyssa, writing in praise of his sister Macrina, says that she "transcended her sex,"⁶ as though she is so impressive because she was thought capable of only so much sanctity as a woman and became more like a man in her exceptional virtue. Men were understood to have a greater natural capacity for virtue than women.

When discussing the difficulty of the pastoral task in *On the Priesthood*, Chrysostom writes, "When it is necessary for someone to lead the Church and be entrusted with the care of so many souls, then let all womanly nature fall back before the magnitude of the work, and most men also."⁷ Part of his task in the treatise is to explain why he ran from ordination, so he explains that it is a big and frightful undertaking to be responsible for souls, so much so that even most men are not up for it, but he says that no

---

5. On efforts at physical beauty as for adultery and prostitution, see *Hom. 1 Cor.* 18.1 (PG 61:148). On beauty as making women more lascivious and men lustful, see *Hom. Jo.* 69.3 (PG 59:380–82).

6. Gregory of Nyssa, *Life of Macrina* 1 (GNO 8.1:345–414). For English translation, see Gregory of Nyssa, *Ascetical Works*, 159–92.

7. *Sac.* 2.2 (SC 172:104–6).

women are up for it at all. They are excluded because their nature is not as strong as that of men.

In his letter to a young widow, early in his career, Chrysostom explains to the widow where her greatest temptations will now be and why she should remain unmarried, even as it will be difficult. Chrysostom writes, "Generally the female sex leans more sensitive to suffering, but when there is also added youth and untimely widowhood and inexperience in business affairs and a great mob of concerns, . . . if she who suffers it does not meet with help from above then even a passing thought will be able to dissolve her."[8] But, says Chrysostom, there is hope because this young widow's fortitude is evidence of God's care for her in keeping her away from vice: "I put it to you that this is the first and greatest sign of many of God's care for you: when such great evils suddenly came together, you were not drowned by grief nor driven out of your natural mind."[9] Her natural condition is weak, but God has strengthened her to not be overwhelmed by grief.

In one of the homilies on Matthew when Chrysostom talks about the monks being an angelic encampment in the desert that congregants should go visit, learn from, and then imitate in the cities, Chrysostom spends a long paragraph explaining how women as well as men are part of this group. In this passage he is describing monks as living "angelic" lives of war with the devil, and he says women also are able to engage the fight against the devil just like the men because this fight is about choice rather than physical nature.[10] All people can become angelic.

On one hand, Chrysostom describes the women being virtuous partly as a way to shame men into choosing a similar

8. *Vid.* 1 (PG 48:599–600).
9. *Vid.* 1 (PG 48:600).
10. *Hom. Matt.* 8.4 (PG 57:87).

ascetic virtue, which shows his understanding that women are somehow weaker than men. His being impressed with the women is in part because his expectations of them are lower. On the other hand, Chrysostom seems to be genuinely applauding these women and making a statement about the equality of women. This is to take his own understanding of moral responsibility seriously and run it to its conclusion. If virtue is about choice rather than nature, and if all people, women included, have been created with this free and self-determining faculty of choice, the women are able to exercise that choice and be virtuous alongside men. Chrysostom does not explain if their weaker nature somehow makes it harder for them to choose virtue, but that may be how he makes sense of the contradiction in his expressed views.

It is also a significant theme that Chrysostom praises female ascetics. The passage we just saw is one example, and others include his praising his friend Olympias, a wealthy widow who gives generously to the church.[11] In his understanding, widows who choose not to remarry are living ascetic lives because of their chastity, and asceticism is the highest calling for a person in Chrysostom's view, so they are women who are praised. It is also worth noting that ascetic was one role for women in the ancient world that was acceptable. People had categories for women living monastic lives and saw them as good, even as saints, because of the renunciations, in a way that married women were not. There were different expectations of each group.

CHRYSOSTOM'S WORDS ABOUT JEWS

The other set of beliefs twenty-first-century Christians should find problematic is about the Jews. Chrysostom's

---

11. John Chrysostom, *Lettres à Olympias*; Ford, *Letters to Saint Olympia*.

anti-Semitism, like that of his contemporaries, tends to be about Jews not having the full story about Jesus and Christians knowing better, or that Jews rejected the truth in rejecting and killing Christ, and therefore the Christians are wiser and have a better and truer understanding of God. In short, Chrysostom thinks Christians are superior to Jews. It is noteworthy that the comments Chrysostom makes about this are always to Christians, not to Jews themselves, and his purpose is not to incite hatred for the Jews or stir up violence but only to convince his people to be Christians rather than Jews. He uses the Jews as a counterpoint to shame Christians into doing or thinking or being better.

Much the way he uses ancient philosophers, Chrysostom uses Jewish beliefs as an apologetic tool. Chrysostom wants his listeners to believe that Christianity is the truth, the right way of belief, and he sets up both philosophers and Jews—in different places—as the foil or setup so he can then say that if the listener thought the Jews had a good idea, the Christians have it even more right. They are merely a step on his way to proof. Chrysostom writes, "The priests of the Jews had the authority to heal bodily leprosy, or, rather, not to heal it but only to approve the healing.... But our priests received authority not over bodily leprosy but over the soul's uncleanness, and not only to approve its healing but to actually heal it."[12] Here his purpose is to explain that anyone who looks down on a Christian priest or does not take them seriously is misguided, for their authority is significant, even more so than the priests of the Jews. This is representative of Chrysostom's discussions of Jews in many places: first he explains what the Jewish belief or custom was, then he shows how the Christian belief or custom is better.

The other way this comes out is that Chrysostom portrays the Jews as childlike. They were undisciplined, or

12. *Sac.* 3.6 (SC 172:152).

requiring discipline to come into line: "When God wanted them to fast, they grew fat; when God did not want them to fast, they fasted contentiously; when he wanted them to offer sacrifices, they ran to idols; when God did not want them to celebrate the feast days, they were eager to celebrate them."[13] Chrysostom also describes Jews as ignorant. In his homily on Psalm 8, Chrysostom explains why God focuses on visible things when communicating with the Jews: "Being thick, they were led from visible things rather than from invisible things. . . . For this reason the discussion is simpler."[14] This is common in Chrysostom. For him, the Jews were more concrete, like children before abstract thought is possible. They are more materialistic rather than spiritual, and as Chrysostom and other late-fourth-century Christians (as well as many modern Christians) believed that spiritual things are superior to material realities, they believed the Jews' thinking was inferior. God had to speak to them like children to help them understand, but God speaks to Christians like adults capable of higher levels of thought.

Though his intent may have been about motivating Christians to believe or behave rightly—rather than direct hatred of Jews—the impact of Chrysostom's rhetoric, along with much of his contemporaries' rhetoric, has been deeply damaging, especially his series of homilies specifically against the Jews.

AGAINST THE JEWS/AGAINST THE JUDAIZING CHRISTIANS

Originally titled *Against the Jews*, many scholars have renamed the series *Against the Judaizing Christians* to reflect its content more accurately, though some prefer to keep

13. *Adv. Jud.* 4.4 (PG 48:876).
14. *Exp. Ps.* 8.6 (PG 55:115).

the original title because the polemic is indeed against the Jews and their practices, even as he is ostensibly chastising Christians for following those practices.[15] One scholar describes this set of homilies this way: "Of the more than 800 of his genuine homilies that survive the relatively tiny cluster that John Chrysostom preached in Antioch against the Jews are among the most quoted, discussed, and contentious."[16] It makes sense. Modern Christians understand the devastating impact Christian anti-Semitism has had on Jews throughout history. Some scholars go the route of trying to explain or exonerate or mitigate Chrysostom's homilies about Jews. Some situate them historically and ask readers to understand the homilies in their own particular context, separate from their impact or use in the medieval and modern periods.[17] The historical work is important, but I am trying here, in addition to noting their context and intent, to acknowledge them, recognize their impact, and decide how to deal with Chrysostom and his works even as I acknowledge the harmful rhetoric about the Jews.

The eight homilies against the Jews address the issue of Christians who wanted to continue to keep Jewish traditions. Preached in Antioch just after his ordination, Chrysostom spoke to his Christian congregation during the Jewish festivals in the city. The audience were Christians who might respect the Jewish way of life and saw no

15. For more on this as well as a helpful overview of the scholarship on this set of homilies, see Mayer, "Preaching Hatred?" Mayer is particularly interested in the impact of these homilies and notes not only the way Chrysostom's homilies were used in the Middle Ages and modernity for anti-Semitic violence but also the impact the homilies likely had in their own time and place.

16. Mayer, "Preaching Hatred?," 58.

17. For a standard work on this, see Wilken, *John Chrysostom and the Jews*.

problem with Christians who attended Jewish festivals and observed Jewish practices, though they themselves did not.

As the title indicates, Chrysostom is against Christians observing Jewish traditions. The homilies are an argument that Christians need to be Christians, not Jews. Jewish practices and traditions became obsolete with Christ, and anyone who follows them is going backward in faith. Chrysostom says that Jewish practices were the way Jews, who were not capable of full understanding of God and God's work in Christ, followed God. But these practices are insufficient. They focus on material things; they are about following laws rather than receiving grace. These practices were God's accommodation to Jews who were not capable of anything more, but Christians have Christ, so more is available to them. They are better off. And to willingly choose the inferior practices is to turn away from the gifts of Christ, who made it possible to be close to God. To willingly choose those inferior practices is to show oneself to be unworthy of Christ's work.

To make his argument, Chrysostom says many inflammatory and insulting things about the Jews. Indeed, Chrysostom's rhetoric in these homilies is some of the worst invective against Jews among ancient Christian authors. Presumably Chrysostom says such awful things to make the position of the Jews much less attractive to the Christians who are considering following them. If he can show Jews to be the worst kind of people, worth hating, then no Christians will be tempted to join them. Chrysostom can thus convince the Christians to stay in their superior place. This is likely the reason the invective in these eight homilies is so much worse than anywhere else in his corpus, where he is not trying to dissuade Christians from joining the Jews.

Regardless of motive, however, Chrysostom still says awful things. One metaphor he uses throughout the series is that of body-illness-cure. The body of the church is ill with the infection of the Judaizers, and they must be cured or kicked out for the body of the church to be cured. He also sometimes talks about Jews and Judaizers themselves as ill with wrong belief, and they could be cured if they but listened and heeded the healing words of Christians. Chrysostom uses this language about heretics in other homilies, notably his homilies on Nicene orthodoxy, *On the Incomprehensible Nature of God*.[18]

Chrysostom cites Jewish weakness as the reason God gave them sacrifices to do in the first place, even though God did not want sacrifices. He proposes the question why God allowed sacrifices from the Jews and answers as if to the Jews themselves:

> He was condescending to your weakness. Just as if a doctor, seeing a man with a fever, impatient and implacable, desiring a drink of cold water and threatening to hang himself if he does not receive it, . . . gives him the lesser evil because he wants to prevent the greater and to lead him away from ending his life.[19]

Chrysostom continues, "This is what God did. Since he saw [the Jews] mad, choking, desiring sacrifices, preparing to desert to idols if they did not receive them. . . . He gave in and let them have sacrifices."[20]

---

18. Harkins, *On the Incomprehensible Nature of God*. Chrysostom says that those members of the congregation who still adhere to a version of Arianism (the Anomeans) are a virus to the body of the church and must be cured of their illness (believing incorrectly), both so they themselves can be whole as well as for the healing of the church body.

19. *Adv. Jud.* 4.6 (PG 48:880).

20. *Adv. Jud.* 4.6 (PG 48:880).

PART 2: CHRYSOSTOM'S THOUGHT

The other major metaphor Chrysostom employs is crime and punishment. The Jews are criminals, primarily for the murder of Christ, and therefore they need to be punished. This plays along with Chrysostom's bent toward justice and fairness. All of the fifth homily against the Jews is about God's destruction of the temple (70 CE) as punishment for the Jews and also an example of God's lovingkindness—he destroys the temple in order to stop their madness, correct them, so they can find eternal salvation by turning to Christ.

Like his views on women, Chrysostom's views on Jews are the views of many powerful men of his time, and they have persisted. There are still narratives among Christians that Jews are criminals because they murdered Christ. Aside from the historical inaccuracy—the Romans executed Christ—these narratives continue to be problematic, and when we read these views from ancients whom we consider to be spiritual giants, we need to know how to interact with their thoughts lest we see in them only support for views that lead us further from holiness rather than closer to it.

WHAT DO WE DO WITH ALL OF THIS?

Blatant ignoring of these themes is not a great option. It is a tempting option, but to refuse to acknowledge that Chrysostom—or any author—has written things that we think are not good, not true, or are even sinful, is to misunderstand the point of confession in Christian tradition. We need to acknowledge these aspects of writing in order to take responsibility for them, to acknowledge that they are untrue or harmful, and thus to exercise humility.[21] In recognizing the

---

21. A friend pointed out that much of the time Chrysostom is following and explaining what he understands to be the message of Scripture, and so Christians also need to reckon with the difficult

sin within Christian tradition, Christians make attempts at truthfulness, to witness to the work of God in restoring the world. Unless a person acknowledges where he is failing or at fault, he cannot participate in the growth in sanctity that God has for him. The same is true of the church as a body. We acknowledge where our tradition has fallen short so that we can learn and grow further in sanctity. To ignore the places where Christians have claimed a vision of the world that is not wholly good is to say that they have no need for growth. It is a prideful posture. Further, acknowledging that Chrysostom says things that are untrue as we understand them, as we now understand God's work and what God says about humanity, also reminds us to hold our own vision of reality loosely and humbly. We might also be wrong or have an incomplete view. Therefore, in reading Chrysostom, we have to acknowledge the existence of these themes.

However, I also do not want to hold up these passages and dimensions of Chrysostom's writing as good or worthy of emulation in the ways that I read other parts of his work. I do not want others to find in them evidence for continuing sexism and anti-Semitism in Christianity. I want to acknowledge these passages, recognize the context they come from, understand the theology they offer, and then be discerning about whether that theology coheres with

---

nature of the Scriptures themselves as well as what people have said about them. There are things written in the Bible about women and Jews (and others) that in certain readings are problematic. How we work with Scripture is also a significant part of the conversation. For one helpful way into this conversation, see C. Smith, *Bible Made Impossible*; and for a good overview of how Scripture has been interpreted throughout history, see Hauser and Watson, *History of Biblical Interpretation* (3 vols.). For an accessible deep dive into how ancients like Chrysostom interpreted the Bible, see O'Keefe and Reno, *Sanctified Vision*.

orthodoxy as I receive it from the tradition and whether it leads me closer to God or further from God.

Really, when we read Christian writers of any century we are always discerning what is useful for our living in the world and growing more into who Christ has made us to be. When I read Chrysostom on asceticism, there are things that I find resonant with truth as I understand it to the best of my ability and there are places where I disagree with him. In this sense, attending to Chrysostom's sexism and anti-Semitism are only heightened examples of this process because of the public nature of how Christian understandings of these ideas have changed in the past two millennia, not a specific problem of their own.

Describing this process of reading is not to say that I may pick and choose what I like from Chrysostom. When I say there are things that are resonant with reality and with God as I understand them, I do not mean things that I like or do not like, or things that are comfortable or uncomfortable. I am not suggesting we run from anything that seems uncomfortable or different from the way we usually conceive God and the world. Chrysostom must challenge me, or I am not listening humbly.

The big question this chapter is really asking, then, is how to read Christian authors. I am arguing—implicitly until now—that reading ancient Christians like Chrysostom offers modern Christians further ways to understand God and their relationship to him. That is, Chrysostom worships the same God that Christians of the twenty-first century worship, and Chrysostom was trying to understand and help his people understand how to live with that God, just like Christians today must do. Therefore, twenty-first-century Christians may read Chrysostom to better understand how to live with God and be transformed into the people God has made them to be, just as they read anyone else in their search for sanctification.

So, dear reader, how do we discern what is useful and what is not? How do we distinguish what is uncomfortable because it is challenging from what is uncomfortable because it is not of God? Though this question applies to more than reading Chrysostom, I am going to stick to discussing Chrysostom in particular and allow readers to draw further conclusions about their own lives and conversations as they wish. The short answer is that if a theology leads closer to God, a person's life will show increased love. Chrysostom, from his own context, says that women are obsessed with finery rather than their souls' virtue. Do I love the characterization of women? No. I know plenty of men who are also obsessed with style and accessories. Should I think of women as all vapid and unconcerned with virtue? No. That is an understanding that loves people less and is, in fact, in contradiction to what Chrysostom says about particular women he admires. Is his point that we should care more about how we dress our souls than our bodies a point that will lead to increased love in my life? Yes. I look at what he is trying to say: our heart matters, our holiness matters, and I should want to be caught up in concern for these things more than I am caught up in concern for things that will pass away. That is a statement that ought to lead to closer union with God. And if I ignore the whole passage because of his views of women, then I miss something useful.

One important way to read people is also to read the whole person, not one part only. Chrysostom's own views on the human person and her moral responsibility and freedom of choice—explored in depth in chapter 5—challenge his views on women and Jews as childlike, vapid, or evil. Everyone has choice; everyone has agency; everyone is capable of virtue. If we ask Chrysostom to take his own commitments seriously, he might have to rethink his position on women and Jews. If adult Jews are human, they have choice and agency and are responsible for their virtue just like adult Christians, and therefore Chrysostom would need to acknowledge that they are not childlike by some kind of nature but are equal human beings in God's world. The same is true of women: if God made all people free and self-determining, with a *proairesis*, then women are just as capable of virtue as men.

It is also important to recognize that whatever we decide about these things will always be incomplete, limited by our own finite existence. We may not get it all "right." The best answers we have may be found to be outdated or wrong in the future. Yet we also have to live and choose. We cannot wait to get it right before living. Therefore, we do the best we can, believe firmly, and hold our understanding loosely enough to admit when we are wrong and accept correction. God knows we do not have it all right; he's waiting for us to acknowledge it so he can work with us to move forward into greater sanctity.

And that greater sanctity is a communal future together where we can imagine that we are changed by each other. I am changed by what I read in Chrysostom, and in the communion of saints, Chrysostom can be changed by conversation with me. Chrysostom himself is insistent on a person's ability to change—again because of his commitment to choice and freedom over nature—so I imagine sitting with him over tea sometime in God's time, and there is possibility that he and I are changed by one another and by all the other people God puts in our world so that we all come together into the heavenly city.

CONCLUSION

Chrysostom was a fourth-century man with power. His views of both women and Jews are consistent with those of his contemporaries. They are also views that have had negative impacts on women and Jews throughout history. Chrysostom says that women are frivolous, caring more about their physical beauty than about their virtue, and more significantly that women are weaker than men, less able to handle life and temptations, even as female ascetics are more impressive for their choosing the rigors of asceticism while being weak women. About Jews Chrysostom is more harmful. To him, Jews are ignorant and childlike, people God put up with and cared about condescendingly but who are inferior because they did not understand who Christ is. Worse, they are criminals and murderers because they murdered Christ. The "contagion" of the Jews must be extracted from the body of the church lest anyone become infected and drawn away from the truth of Christ.

These are Chrysostom's views, and they are not views modern Christians ought to perpetuate, even as some do. I opened the chapter with a question about statues and whether we can or should judge historical people's thoughts by our own time, and I have tried to show how complex that question is.[22] In the end, I will not be advocating for any Chrysostom statues, and not only because he would be appalled (humility was a big deal for those we've labeled saints in ancient Christianity). Chrysostom is still worthy of being listened to about many things, but acknowledging the places where his views lead away from more holiness in

22. I have only discussed the issues regarding how we think about ancient figures' thoughts and beliefs. There are many other sets of issues in the statues controversies about politics, power, and historical and ongoing struggles that are also important to work through, but that is not what this chapter has been about.

God (as we understand it now) is important for humility. We can acknowledge that saintly Christians' views might not all be saintly views. Significantly, we can say this because we worship the same God and read the same Scriptures in attempts to come closer to and better emulate that God. We recognize these views, we sort through what is useful for growth in holiness, and we forgive the rest, working to do better so that the whole body of Christ continues to cooperate with God in his work of transforming us into greater Christlikeness.

DISCUSSION QUESTIONS

1. What are views you once held that you've changed your mind about? What brought about the change?
2. What are your guidelines for reading things you disagree with? How do you engage with what you read and open yourself to be changed by it while also acknowledging what seems far from God in it?
3. Acknowledging that Chrysostom's views are problematic, what are some of the deeper truths we can learn from him still in our modern context?
4. What is significant about the context in which Chrysostom preached his sermons that are now regarded as anti-Semitic?

CONCLUSION

JOHN CHRYSOSTOM'S LIFE IN the fourth century was one of intensity. Trained as a classical rhetorician but convinced by the Christian faith, he was baptized and lived with commitment to this faith. His goal was to be an ascetic, which at the time he believed to be the most faithful form of the Christian life. Ascetics had to give up everything and spend every moment in prayer and contemplation of God, living without the distractions and comforts of city life. Chrysostom succeeded as a monk—such an intense personality was built for extreme devotion—for a few years before his health forced him to return to the city of Antioch, where officials ordained him to the priesthood.

In the pulpit Chrysostom earned his nickname, "Golden Mouth," because of his eloquence. Preaching to congregants several times a week, his skill in explaining Scripture to the listeners and speaking persuasively had the attention of church authorities, and in 397 CE, they ordained him bishop of Constantinople. Here Chrysostom continued his preaching at Hagia Sophia, the imperial church, as well as taking up all the ecclesiastical duties of a bishop. In spite of his position, Chrysostom held to his monastic ideals and was uncompromising when dealing with clergy under his care. Not only did he preach strict morality to his congregants, but Chrysostom refused to eat with dignitaries as was expected of the bishop and did not bow to imperial pressures. The emperor and empress attended his church, and Chrysostom expected them to abide by Christian virtue in their dealings and lives because he understood their faith to be a higher authority than their political authority.

It is not surprising, then, that Chrysostom's zeal caused friction with some imperial and ecclesiastical authorities. Though his audiences loved him, it is unclear how much impact on daily living his persuasion had, whether laity really did live with more virtue under his constant exhortations. What is clear is that Theophilus, bishop of Alexandria, did not respect Chrysostom or share his parishioners' enthusiasm for his leadership. Theophilus spearheaded the Synod of the Oak, after Chrysostom gave refuge to some persecuted monks from Theophilus's jurisdiction, and through some political machinations succeeded in having Chrysostom exiled from Constantinople. Briefly recalled to the city after protests from Christians in the city, Chrysostom was eventually exiled a second time. While in exile he carried on a correspondence with his dear friend Olympias, so we know that he suffered severely in physical ways, but he still wrote with encouragement and attempted to imitate the blessed apostle Paul in his acceptance of suffering. Eventually the pace and weather of his exile caught up to him, and he died in 407 CE.

Throughout his career, Chrysostom came back to a few themes repeatedly, and so as much as I have introduced Chrysostom through his biography, I have also in this book attempted to introduce him through his thought. I began with a discussion of his pastoral theology because it helps one to understand how he went about his preaching work. To Chrysostom, the priest's work in expounding Scripture and persuading people to virtuous lives was the primary work they do. He considered the priest both a guardian and a physician: protecting the congregation from heresy and offering the words of Scripture like medicine, needing to know the appropriate dose at the appropriate time. Priestly work was extremely skilled work, and Chrysostom excelled at it.

Another theme Chrysostom returned to frequently was asceticism and the superiority of ascetic forms of living, whether or not a person embraced a complete withdrawal from society. Sometime after Chrysostom returned to the city and worked in his ecclesiastical roles, we see him acknowledge that though asceticism is the most faithful way of life, he no longer believes that living in the mountains as a celibate is more faithful than living asceticism in the city as a married person. Chrysostom increasingly insists that all people can live like the monks do, with self-restraint, detached from worldly things (in *apatheia*), and focused on contemplation of God, even as they have spouses and jobs in the city. It will be more difficult, Chrysostom says, because of the many extra distractions city life involves, but it is possible and indeed is the way of flourishing and virtue God desires for his people. This detachment from the world is what Adam and Eve had in the garden of Eden and what they lost when they disobeyed God's order. This detachment is what the monks recover and what all people ought to aim for because it is the way of flourishing in friendship with God.

Chrysostom also says that this way of life is attainable for everyone because God has created every human being with a *proairesis*, a capacity for choice, that is free and self-determining. No one—not even the devil or God—can force a person to do anything. Everything is a choice. If an act were not a free choice, then the person doing the act could be neither praised nor blamed for it. Since Chrysostom is committed to the idea that God is just, then God's punishment or reward of actions must be just and therefore each person must be morally responsible because of a free capacity for choice. All of this is to say that virtue, living in ways that God has asked people to live, is each person's choice and responsibility, and because it is a choice, Chrysostom says every person can attain it. Everyone can choose to live in the ascetic ways that bring about flourishing.

Much of the time Chrysostom only tells his congregants to be virtuous in general terms, but one virtue that he names over and over is almsgiving. To provide for the poor is essential, and Chrysostom questions whether a Christian can justly own wealth. In theory Christians can be wealthy, if they use their wealth properly, but Chrysostom spends so much time telling people to give everything away that he seems to think having wealth means a person is not using it properly. Moreover, Chrysostom often speaks of almsgiving as salvific. Give alms to beggars, who stand in for Christ, and receive heaven, he says. One reason for this, I think, is that Chrysostom sees wealth as a distraction from a Christian's focus on God. Almsgiving is an ascetic practice, a stripping of distraction, just like fasting or vigils. Thus almsgiving is part of the work to be virtuous. One other thing Chrysostom's emphasis on almsgiving suggests to me is that Chrysostom's vision of a heavenly city is one where everyone has what they need. The vision for salvation is communal, not individual, even as individuals have moral responsibility.

Salvation is ultimately the reason that Chrysostom emphasizes each person's responsibility for virtue so strongly. Chrysostom understands salvation to be a cooperative venture between God and the Christian. God has done all the heavy lifting already—Christ's incarnation, death, and resurrection—but a person has to bring both her faith and her virtue to add to God's work in order to participate in her salvation. God is transforming the cities of earth into heavenly cities, and everyone participates. They must bring their virtue both for their own sake, to show that they are earnest about their salvation, as well as for the sake of the whole community, because only when everyone is living in virtue is the whole city living in virtue and the ways God has intended for human flourishing.

Finally, as important as so much of Chrysostom's thought is for Christians still today, it is important to recognize that some of Chrysostom's thoughts are not faithful, especially his views on women and Jews. Christians must acknowledge where we have led people further from God, so we need to acknowledge these aspects of Chrysostom's thought, rather than ignore them, and we also need ways to say that they are not of God. The final chapter was an attempt to read Chrysostom's work as a whole and complex corpus, noting where his own thought ought to lead him in a different direction but where he has serious prejudice I do not want to imitate. I suggest that we consider him as a whole person with a range of thoughts and take him as a conversation partner, hoping that we challenge and change each other in the communion of saints. We listen for what is of God and what is not of God. But theological conversations of any time are difficult, so we also take a posture of humility, recognizing that our own ideas are also incomplete and open to be challenged by Christians of another time and place.

That conversation among the communion of saints has been the reason for this book. John Chrysostom is one of the Christians from another time and place with whom we are in communion. He is someone from whom we can learn, someone who did his best to follow Christ and whose wisdom has been marked by the church as worth listening to. It can be hard to see the blind spots in our own culture, but listening to someone who worships the same God from a different place and time can help.

Chrysostom's emphasis on personal moral responsibility can be helpful when we talk about responsibility, blame, or ethics. Our present moment in the United States sees us in an all-or-nothing intensity when it comes to behavior. Different groups talk about ideas and actions that are acceptable or not acceptable, and we demonize our opponents, talk about each other and our ideas like viruses that infect. Chrysostom, a fairly black-and-white preacher himself, says not to fear one another, not to cut each other off but to work for everyone to be part of the transformed city. Most significantly, Chrysostom says one should pay attention to one's own moral responsibility more than to one's neighbor's. We cannot force our neighbor to do anything, but we are able to make our own choices freely, and we must. If we attend to our own virtue first and are less concerned with our neighbor's, we might see each other as people doing our best and be willing to find some way forward together instead of cutting each other off, especially if salvation is a communal reality.

Similarly, I find Chrysostom's insistence on asceticism as a way of life, even in the midst of daily distractions, a faithful challenge. He does not allow me to say that monks have this call and I am allowed to live a little more loosely. No, Chrysostom says that I am responsible for attending to my attachments too, right where I am, and it might even be harder. I have to recognize when I eat too much because eating is comforting when I am overwhelmed by my emotions. I have to notice when I put off going to bed because watching a little more TV is easier than facing the thoughts in my head. I have to pay attention to how much screen

Conclusion

time is keeping me from prayer. God wants friendship with me, says Chrysostom, and I am attached to things that will dissolve that friendship rather than attach me to God. Moreover, by holding things loosely, I will be less thrown by the struggles that inevitably come with living. I will be more able to stay with God in some kind of calm, even in the midst of suffering.

In a world obsessed by money and a place especially affected by inflation, Chrysostom challenges me to give more than I receive, to give to those who need rather than hoard what I have because I fear it will disappear too soon. Or in a world that says wealth is another of God's blessings and if we just live faithfully God will provide, Chrysostom tells me that wealth is just another external circumstance that has no bearing on my virtue apart from what I do with it. In fact, it will be harder to be faithful if I have it. But I ought not look at the poor man on the street corner and assume he deserves to be there, or assume that God loves him less, or that he has somehow lived unfaithfully and that is why he struggles to feed himself.

Chrysostom is full of challenges, but he is also full of encouragement. He tells me that God is standing with me in the arena as I fight to live faithfully. Christ has rigged the contest and sets me back on my feet when I fall; he does not taunt or punish me for failure. Indeed, Christ has chosen to marry me and transform me into a true beauty. Chrysostom says that working toward virtue is virtue enough. He emphasizes that Christ has done all the hard work to bring me close, and all I have to do is make one choice after another to cooperate and I can come as close as I am willing.

John Chrysostom, dead now sixteen hundred years, is my friend. He tells me to have hope, and he tells me to watch myself. He points the way to Christ. He lets me read Scripture over his shoulder and see things I didn't know were

Conclusion

there. My hope is that in this introduction Chrysostom has had some words for you as well. I hope he has become a little more familiar to you, perhaps become someone you might seek out for further conversation. Perhaps one day we will all sit at a café in the heavenly city and enjoy some wine and lively conversation together.

BIBLIOGRAPHY

PRIMARY SOURCES

Chrysostom, Critical Editions

A Theodore. Edited by Jean Dumortier. Sources chrétiennes 117. Paris: Cerf, 1966.
Commentaire sur Job. Edited by Henri Sorlin and Louis Neyrand. Sources chrétiennes 346. Paris: Cerf, 1988.
Lettres à Olympias. Edited by Anne Marie Malingrey. Sources chrétiennes 13. Paris: Cerf, 1968.
Lettre d'exil à Olympias et à tous les fidèles (Quod nemo laeditur). Edited by Anne Marie Malingrey. Sources chrétiennes 103. Paris: Cerf, 1964.
Homélies sur l'impuissance du diable. Edited by Adina Peleanu. Sources chrétiennes 560. Paris: Cerf, 2013.
Huit Catéchèses Baptismales. Edited by Antoine Wenger. Sources chrétiennes 50. Paris: Cerf, 1957.
Sur le sacerdoce: dialogue et homélie. Edited by Anne Marie Malingrey. Sources chrétiennes 272. Paris: Cerf, 1980.
Sur l'incompréhensibilité de Dieu. 2e éd. Edited by Jean Daniélou, Anne Marie Malingrey, and Robert Flacelière. Sources chrétiennes 28. Paris: Cerf, 1970.

Greek of Chrysostom for which there is no critical edition comes from the PG:

Patrologia graeca. Edited by J.-P. Migne. 162 vols. Paris, 1857–86. http://phoenix.reltech.org/Ebind/docs/Migne/Migne.html.

Translations of Chrysostom's Works

Christo, Gus, trans. *On Repentance and Almsgiving*. Fathers of the Church 96. Washington, DC: The Catholic University of America Press, 1998.

Ford, David C., trans. *Letters to Saint Olympia*. Crestwood, NY: St. Vladimir's Seminary Press, 2017.

Habib, John, trans. *On Repentance and Defeating Despair: Letters to Theodore by St. John Chrysostom*. Sandia, TX: St. Mary and St. Moses Abbey, 2018.

Hall, Christopher A. "John Chrysostom's 'On Providence': A Translation and Theological Interpretation." PhD diss., Drew University, Madison, NJ, 1996.

Harkins, Paul W., trans. *Baptismal Instructions*. Ancient Christian Writers 31. Westminster, MD: Newman, 1963.

———, trans. *Discourses Against Judaizing Christians*. Fathers of the Church 68. Washington, DC: The Catholic University of America Press, 1979.

———, trans. *On the Incomprehensible Nature of God*. Fathers of the Church 72. Washington, DC: The Catholic University of America Press, 1984.

Hill, Robert C. *St. John Chrysostom Commentary on Job*. St. John Chrysostom: Commentaries on the Sages, vol. 1. Brookline, MA: Holy Cross Orthodox, 2006.

———. *St. John Chrysostom Commentary on the Psalms*. Vol. 1. Brookline, MA: Holy Cross Orthodox, 1998.

Hunter, David G., trans. *A Comparison Between a King and a Monk; Against the Opponents of the Monastic Life: Two Treatises*. Studies in the Bible and Early Christianity 13. Lewiston, NY: Mellen, 1988.

Neville, Graham, trans. *Six Books on the Priesthood*. Crestwood, NY: St. Vladimir's Seminary Press, 1977.

Roth, Catherine P., trans. *On Wealth and Poverty*. Crestwood, NY: St. Vladimir's Seminary Press, 1984.

Bibliography

All other translations found in:

Schaff, Philip, et al., eds. *A Select Library of the Nicene and Post-Nicene Fathers of the Christian Church*, First Series. 14 vols. Repr., Grand Rapids: Eerdmans, 1956.

Other Primary Sources

Gregory of Nyssa. *Oratio Catechetica: Opera Dogmatica Minora, Pars IV*. Edited by Ekkehard Muhlenberg. Gregorii Nysseni Opera, vol. 3, pt. 4. Leiden: Brill, 1996.
———. *Vita S. Macrinae: Opera Ascetica*. Edited by Virginia Woods Callahan. Gregorii Nysseni Opera, vol. 8, pt. 1. Leiden: Brill, 1963.
Methodius. *Le De autexusio de Méthode d'Olympe: Version slave et texte grec*. Edited by André Vaillant. Patrologia Orientalis 22, fasc. 5. Paris: Firmin-Didot, 1930.
Palladius. *Dialogue sur la vie de Jean Chrysostome*. Edited by Anne-Marie Malingrey. 2 vols. Sources chrétiennes 341 and 342. Paris: Cerf, 1988.
Socrates of Constantinople. *Histoire ecclésiastique: IV–VI*. Edited by Pierre Maraval. Vol. 3. Sources chrétiennes 505. Paris: Cerf, 2004.
Sozomen. *Histoire ecclésiastique: Livres VII–IX*. Edited by Bernard Grillet. Vol. 4. Sources chrétiennes 516. Paris: Cerf, 2008.
Wallraff, M., ed. *Ps.-Martyrius: Oratio funebris in laudem sancti Iohannis Chrysostomi (Ps.-Martyrius Antiochenus, BHG 871, CPG 6517)*. Quaderni della Rivista di Bizantinistica 12. Spoleto: Fondazione Centro Italiano di Studi sull'alto Medioevo, 2007.

Translations of Other Primary Sources

Barnes, Timothy D., and George Bevans, eds. *The Funerary Speech for John Chrysostom*. Translated Texts for Historians 60. Liverpool: Liverpool University Press, 2013.
Basil the Great. *Address to Young Men on Greek Literature*. In *Basil the Great: Letters IV*, translated by Joseph Deferrai and Martin R. P. McGuire, 363–436. Loeb Classical Library 270. Cambridge, MA: Harvard University Press, 1970.
Gregory of Nyssa. *Saint Gregory of Nyssa: Ascetical Works*. Edited and translated by Virginia Woods Callahan. Fathers of the Church

58. Washington, DC: The Catholic University of America Press, 1967.

———. *Catechetical Discourse: A Handbook for Catechists*. Translated by Ignatius Green. Crestwood, NY: St Vladimir's Seminary Press, 2019.

Libanius. *Selected Orations, Volume II: Orations 2*. Edited and translated by A. F. Norman. Loeb Classical Library 452. Cambridge, MA: Harvard University Press, 1977.

Palladius. *Palladius: Dialogue on the Life of St. John Chrysostom*. Translated by Robert T. Meyer. Ancient Christian Writers 45. Westminster, MD: Newman, 1985.

Methodius found in:

Roberts, Alexander, et al., eds. *A Select Library of the Ante Nicene Fathers of the Christian Church*. 10 vols. Repr., Grand Rapids: Eerdmans, 1969.

Socrates and Sozomen found in:

Schaff, Philip, et al., eds. *A Select Library of the Nicene and Post-Nicene Fathers of the Christian Church*, Second Series. Grand Rapids: Eerdmans, 1979.

SECONDARY SOURCES

Ang, Beatrice Victoria. "Examining John Chrysostom's Ideal of the Ascetic Priest." *Studia Patristica* 128 (2021) 349–62.

Baur, Chrysostomus. *John Chrysostom and His Time*. Translated by M. Gonzaga. 2 vols. Westminster, MD: Newman, 1959.

Barnard, Lawrence R. "Christology and Soteriology in the Preaching of John Chrysostom." ThD diss., Southwestern Baptist Theological Seminary, Dallas, 1974.

Berardino, Angelo Di, et al., eds. *Encyclopedia of Ancient Christianity*. 3 vols. Downers Grove, IL: IVP Academic, 2014.

Bizzell, Patricia, and Bruce Herzberg, eds. *The Rhetorical Tradition: Readings from Classical Times to the Present*. 2nd ed. Boston: Bedford/St. Martin's, 2001.

Bibliography

Brown, Peter. *The Body and Society: Men, Women, and Sexual Renunciation in Early Christianity.* New York: Columbia University Press, 1988.

———. *Poverty and Leadership in the Later Roman Empire.* The Menahem Stern Jerusalem Lectures. Hanover, MD: University Press of New England, 2002.

———. *Treasure in Heaven: The Holy Poor in Early Christianity.* Charlottesville, VA: University of Virginia Press, 2016.

Carpenter, Anne M. *Nothing Gained Is Eternal: A Theology of Tradition.* Minneapolis: Fortress, 2022.

Cribiore, Raffaella. *The School of Libanius in Late Antique Antioch.* Princeton, NJ: Princeton University Press, 2007.

De Wet, Chris L., and Wendy Mayer, eds. *Revisioning John Chrysostom: New Approaches, New Perspectives.* Leiden: Brill, 2019.

Douglas, Bobby. "Easy Virtue: The Intersection of Chrysostom's Pneumatology and Anthropology." ThD diss., Duke University Divinity School, Durham, NC, 2024.

Florovsky, Georges. "St John Chrysostom: The Prophet of Charity." *St Vladimir's Seminary Quarterly* 3 (1955) 37–42.

Gonzalez, Justo. *The Story of Christianity.* Vol. 1: *The Early Church to the Dawn of the Reformation.* New York: HarperOne, 2010.

Hartney, Aideen M. *John Chrysostom and the Transformation of the City.* London: Duckworth, 2004.

Hauser, Alan W., and Duane F. Watson, eds. *A History of Biblical Interpretation.* 3 vols. Grand Rapids: Eerdmans, 2008.

Heine, Ronald E. *Classical Christian Doctrine: Introducing the Essentials of the Ancient Faith.* Grand Rapids: Baker Academic, 2013.

Kelly, J. N. D. *Golden Mouth: The Story of John Chrysostom, Ascetic, Preacher, Bishop.* London: Duckworth, 1995.

Kennedy, George Alexander, trans. *Progymnasmata: Greek Textbooks of Prose Composition and Rhetoric.* Atlanta: Society of Biblical Literature, 2003.

Lai, Pak-Wah. "John Chrysostom: Vision of the Angelic Life." In *Sources of the Christian Self: A Cultural History of Christian Identity*, edited by James M. Houston and Jens Zimmermann, 192–208. Grand Rapids: Eerdmans, 2018.

———. "The Monk as Christian Saint and Exemplar in St John Chrysostom's Writings." In *Saints and Sanctity*, edited by Peter D. Clarke, 19–28. Studies in Church History. Rochester, NY: Boydell, 2011.

Laistner, Max. *Christianity and Pagan Culture in the Later Roman Empire; Together with an English Translation of John Chrysostom's*

Address on Vainglory and the Right Way for Parents to Bring Up Their Children. New York: Cornell University Press, 1951.

Lawrenz, Melvin Edward. "The Christology of John Chrysostom." PhD diss., Marquette University, Milwaukee, WI, 1987.

Leyerle, Blake. *The Narrative Shape of Emotion in the Preaching of John Chrysostom*. Oakland, CA: University of California Press, 2020.

Liebeschuetz, J. H. W. G. *Antioch*. Oxford: Oxford University Press, 1972.

———. *Barbarians and Bishops: Army, Church, and State in the Age of Arcadius and Chrysostom*. With American Council of Learned Societies. Oxford: Oxford University Press, 1990.

Louth, Andrew, ed. *The Oxford Dictionary of the Christian Church*. 4th ed. Oxford: Oxford University Press, 2022.

Mayer, Wendy. "Doing Violence to the Image of an Empress: The Destruction of Eudoxia's Reputation." In *Violence in Late Antiquity: Perceptions and Practices*, edited by H. A. Drake, 205–13. London: Routledge, 2006.

———. "John Chrysostom: Extraordinary Preacher, Ordinary Audience." In *Preacher and Audience*, 105–37. Leiden: Brill, 1998.

———. "John Chrysostom and Women Revisited." In *Men and Women in the Early Christian Centuries*, edited by Wendy Mayer and Ian J. Elmer, 211–25. Strathfield, NSW: St. Paul's Press, 2014.

———. "The Persistence in Late Antiquity of Medico-Philosophical Psychic Therapy." *Journal of Late Antiquity* 8 (2015) 337–51.

———. "Poverty and Generosity Toward the Poor in the Time of John Chrysostom." In *Wealth and Poverty in Early Church and Society*, edited by Susan R. Holman, 140–58. Grand Rapids: Baker Academic, 2008.

———. "Preaching Hatred? John Chrysostom, Neuroscience, and the Jews." In *Revisioning John Chrysostom: New Approaches, New Perspectives*, edited by Chris L. De Wet and Wendy Mayer, 58–136. Critical Approaches to Early Christianity 1. Leiden: Brill, 2019.

———. "Shaping the Sick Soul: Reshaping the Identity of John Chrysostom." In *Christians Shaping Identity from the Roman Empire to Byzantium: Studies Inspired by Pauline Allen*, edited by Wendy Mayer and Geoffrey Dunn, 140–64. Leiden: Brill, 2015.

———. "What Does It Mean to Say That John Chrysostom Was a Monk?" *Studia Patristica* 39 (2006) 451–55.

Meyer, Louis. *Saint Jean Chrysostome, maître de perfection chrétienne*. Paris: Beauchesne, 1933.

Bibliography

Miller, Samantha L. *Chrysostom's Devil: Demons, the Will, and Virtue in Patristic Soteriology*. Downers Grove, IL: IVP Academic, 2020.

———. "The Hellish Homiletic Practices of John Chrysostom and Billy Graham." *Worship* 90 (2017) 300–317.

———. *John Chrysostom and African Charismatic Theology in Conversation: Salvation, Deliverance, and the Prosperity Gospel*. Lanham, MD: Lexington, 2021.

Mitchell, Margaret M. *The Heavenly Trumpet: John Chrysostom and the Art of Pauline Interpretation*. Tübingen: Mohr Siebeck, 2000.

———. "John Chrysostom." In *The Sermon on the Mount Through the Centuries*, edited by Jeffrey P. Greenman, Timothy Larsen, and Stephen R. Spencer, 19–42. Grand Rapids: Brazos, 2007.

Moore, Peter C. "Bound Together for Heaven: Mutual Emotions in Chrysostom's Homilies on Matthew for Well-Ordered and Fruitful Community in Anxious Times." In *Revisioning Chrysostom: New Approaches, New Perspectives*, edited by Chris L. De Wet and Wendy Mayer, 334–60. Critical Approaches to Early Christianity 1. Leiden: Brill, 2019.

O'Keefe, John J., and R. R. Reno. *Sanctified Vision: An Introduction to Early Christian Interpretation of the Bible*. Baltimore: Johns Hopkins University Press, 2005.

Papadogiannakis, Yannis. "Homiletics and the History of Emotions: The Case of John Chrysostom." In *Revisioning Chrysostom: New Approaches, New Perspectives*, edited by Chris L. De Wet and Wendy Mayer, 300–333. Critical Approaches to Early Christianity 1. Leiden: Brill, 2019.

Pradels, W., R. Brändle, and M. Heimgartner. "Das bisher vermisste Textstück in Johannes Chrysostomus, Adversus Judaeos, Oratio 2." *Zeitschrift für Antikes Christentum* 5 (2001) 23–49.

Rhee, Helen. *Loving the Poor, Saving the Rich: Wealth, Poverty, and Early Christian Formation*. Grand Rapids: Baker Academic, 2012.

Rylaarsdam, David. *John Chrysostom on Divine Pedagogy: The Coherence of His Theology and Preaching*. Oxford: Oxford University Press, 2014.

Smith, Christian. *The Bible Made Impossible: Why Biblicism Is Not a Truly Evangelical Reading of Scripture*. Grand Rapids: Brazos, 2012.

Smith, G. A. "How Thin Is a Demon?" *Journal of Early Christian Studies* 16 (2008) 479–512.

Walsh, Efthalia Makris. "Overcoming Gender: Virgins, Widows and Barren Women in the Writings of St. John Chrysostom, 386–397." PhD diss., The Catholic University of America, Washington, DC, 1994.

Bibliography

Wilken, Robert Louis. *John Chrysostom and the Jews: Rhetoric and Reality in the Late 4th Century*. Berkeley: University of California Press, 1983.

INDEX OF CHRYSOSTOM'S WORKS

Adv. Jud., 33, 130, 133

Catech. illum., 77–79, 85–86, 115, 125
Comm. Job, 97
Comp. reg. mon., 63–64, 104

Diab., 4, 54, 80

Eleem., 92, 102–3, 105
Ep. Olymp., 23
Exp. Ps., 130

Hom. 1 Cor., 33, 73, 93, 126
Hom. 2 Cor., 110
Hom. Col., 125
Hom. Eph., 109
Hom. Gal., 50
Hom. Gen., 12, 16, 19, 70, 72, 107, 112, 113, 116, 120
Hom. Heb., 3, 108

Hom. Jo., 19, 80, 87, 88, 111, 126
Hom. Matt., 65, 66, 71, 82, 86, 104, 114, 127
Hom. Phil., 96
Hom. Rom., 33, 72, 108, 118
Hom. 1 Tim., 94

Laed., 83, 86, 88
Laz., 3, 26, 36, 68, 93–94, 97, 102

Oppugn., 63–64, 66, 67, 104

Paenit., 57, 92, 98–100

Sac., 45–49, 51–54, 59, 126, 129
Scand., 56
Stat., 17, 65, 88

Vid., 127

www.ingramcontent.com/pod-product-compliance
Lightning Source LLC
Chambersburg PA
CBHW030858170426
43193CB00009BA/654